studysync®

Reading & Writing Companion

Chasing the Impossible

What makes a dream worth pursuing?

studysync.com

Send all inquiries to:
BookheadEd Learning, LLC
610 Daniel Young Drive
Sonoma, CA 95476

ISBN 978-1-94-469581-1

4 5 6 LMN 24 23 22 21 20

B

Student Guide

Getting Started

Welcome to the StudySync Reading & Writing Companion! In this book, you will find a collection of readings based on the theme of the unit you are studying. As you work through the readings, you will be asked to answer questions and perform a variety of tasks designed to help you closely analyze and understand each text selection. Read on for an explanation of each

Close Reading and Writing Routine

In each unit, you will read texts that share a common theme, despite their different genres, time periods, and authors. Each reading encourages a closer look through questions and a short writing assignment.

Rikki-Tikki-Tavi
FICTION
Rudyard Kipling
1894

① Introduction

studysync●

"Rikki-Tikki-Tavi" is one of the most famous tales from *The Jungle Book*, a collection of short stories published in 1894 by English author Rudyard Kipling (1865–1936). The stories in *The Jungle Book* feature animal characters with anthropomorphic traits and are intended to be read as fables, each illustrating a moral lesson. In this story, Rikki-tikki-tavi is a courageous young mongoose adopted as a pet by a British family living in 19th-century colonial India.

① Introduction

An Introduction to each text provides historical context for your reading as well as information about the author. You will also learn about the genre of the text and the year in which it was written.

② Notes

Many times, while working through the activities after each text, you will be asked to **annotate** or **make annotations** about what you are reading. This means that you should highlight or underline words in the text and use the "Notes" column to make comments or jot down any questions you have. You may also want to note any unfamiliar vocabulary words here.

You will also see sample student annotations to go along with the Skill lesson for that text.

Rikki-Tikki-Tavi

"Rikki-tikki held on with his eyes shut, for now he was quite sure he was dead."

1 This is the story of the great war that Rikki-tikki-tavi fought single-handed, through the bath-rooms of the big bungalow in Segowlee cantonment. Darzee, the Tailorbird, helped him, and Chuchundra, the musk-rat, who never comes out into the middle of the floor, but always creeps round by the wall, gave him advice, but Rikki-tikki did the real fighting.

2 He was a mongoose, rather like a little cat in his fur and his tail, but quite like a weasel in his head and his habits. His eyes and the end of his restless nose were pink. He could scratch himself anywhere he pleased with any leg, front or back, that he chose to use. He could fluff up his tail till it looked like a bottle brush, and his war cry as he scuttled through the long grass was: "Rikk-tikk-tikki-tikki-tchk!"

3 One day, a high summer flood washed him out of the burrow where he lived with his father and mother, and carried him, kicking and clucking, down a roadside ditch. He found a little wisp of grass floating there, and clung to it till he lost his senses. When he revived, he was lying in the hot sun on the middle of a garden path, very draggled indeed, and a small boy was saying, "Here's a dead mongoose. Let's have a funeral."

4 "No," said his mother, "let's take him in and dry him. Perhaps he isn't really dead."

5 They took him into the house, and a big man picked him up between his finger and thumb and said he was not dead but half choked. So they wrapped him in cotton wool, and warmed him over a little fire, and he opened his eyes and sneezed.

6 "Now," said the big man (he was an Englishman who had just moved into the bungalow), "don't frighten him, and we'll see what he'll do."

Skill
Textual Evidence

It says that he fluffs up his tail and he has a war cry. I know that a war cry is used in battle to rally the troops. This must mean that Rikki-tikki is brave and powerful, like a soldier.

Skill
Text-Dependent Responses

After finding Rikki-tikki, the English family brought him into their home and took care of him.

Reading & Writing Companion

First Read

During your first reading of each selection, you should just try to get a general idea of the content and message of the reading. Don't worry if there are parts you don't understand or words that are unfamiliar to you. You'll have an opportunity later to dive deeper into the text.

Think Questions

These questions will ask you to start thinking critically about the text, asking specific questions about its purpose, and making connections to your prior knowledge and reading experiences. To answer these questions, you should go back to the text and draw upon specific evidence to support your responses. You will also begin to explore some of the more challenging vocabulary words in the selection.

Skills

Each Skill includes two parts: Checklist and Your Turn. In the Checklist, you will learn the process for analyzing the text. The model student annotations in the text provide examples of how you might make your own notes following the instructions in the Checklist. In the Your Turn, you will use those same instructions to practice the skill.

3

RIKKI-TIKKI-TAVI
studysync

First Read

Read "Rikki-Tikki-Tavi." After you read, complete the Think Questions below.

4

THINK QUESTIONS

1. How did Rikki-tikki come to live with the English family? Cite specific evidence from the text to support your answer.

2. What do the descriptions of Nag and the dialogue in paragraphs 23–24 suggest about Nag's character? Cite specific evidence from the text to support your answer.

3. Describe in two to three sentences how Rikki-tikki saves the family from snakes.

4. Find the word **cultivated** in paragraph 18 of "Rikki-Tikki-Tavi." Use context clues in the surrounding sentences, as well as the sentence in which the word appears, to determine the word's meaning. Write your definition here and identify clues that helped you figure out the word's meaning.

5. Use context clues to determine the meaning of **sensible** as it is used in paragraph 79 of "Rikki-Tikki-Tavi." Write your definition of *sensible* here and identify clues that helped you figure out the meaning. Then check the meaning in the dictionary.

5

CHARACTER

Skill:
Character

Use the Checklist to analyze Character in "Rikki-Tikki-Tavi." Refer to the sample student annotations about Character in the text.

••• CHECKLIST FOR CHARACTER

In order to determine how particular elements of a story or drama interact, note the following:

✓ the characters in the story, including the protagonist and antagonist

✓ the settings and how they shape the characters or plot

✓ plot events and how they affect the characters

✓ key events or series of episodes in the plot, especially events that cause characters to react, respond, or change in some way

✓ characters' responses as the plot reaches a climax and moves toward a resolution of the problem facing the protagonist

✓ the resolution of the conflict in the plot and the ways that affects each character

To analyze how particular elements of a story or drama interact, consider the following questions:

✓ How do the characters' responses change or develop from the beginning to the end of the story?

✓ How does the setting shape the characters and plot in the story?

✓ How do the events in the plot affect the characters? How do they develop as a result of the conflict, climax, and resolution?

✓ Do the characters' problems reach a resolution? How?

⟳ YOUR TURN

5

1. How does the mother's love for her son affect her actions in paragraph 37?

  ○ A. It prompts her to keep her son away from Rikki-tikki.
  ○ B. It causes a disagreement between her and her husband.
  ○ C. It makes her show affection towards Rikki-tikki.
  ○ D. It makes Rikki-tikki feel nervous staying with the family.

2. What does the dialogue in paragraph 40 suggest about Chuchundra?

  ○ A. He is afraid.
  ○ B. He is easily fooled.
  ○ C. He is optimistic.
  ○ D. He loves Rikki-tikki.

3. Which paragraph shows that Teddy looks to Rikki-tikki for protection?

  ○ A. 37
  ○ B. 38
  ○ C. 39
  ○ D. 40

Close Read

6

Reread "Rikki-Tikki-Tavi." As you reread, complete the Skills Focus questions below. Then use your answers and annotations from the questions to help you complete the Write activity.

SKILLS FOCUS

1. Identify details that reveal Nag's character when he is first introduced in the story. Explain what inferences you can make about Nag and what makes him a threat.

2. Identify details that reveal Rikki-tikki's character traits as a fighter. Explain how those character traits help Rikki-tikki defeat the snakes.

3. Find examples of Nag and Nagaina's actions and dialogue. How do their words and behaviors create conflict in the plot?

4. Identify details that help you compare and contrast Rikki-tikki and Darzee. Explain what you can infer about Rikki-tikki and Darzee from these details.

5. Analyze details that show how Rikki-tikki beats the snakes. Explain Rikki-tikki's approach to conflict.

✏ WRITE

7

LITERARY ANALYSIS: In this classic story of good vs. evil, Nag and Nagaina are portrayed as the villains. Consider the role and behaviors of the typical villain. Then think about Nag and Nagaina's behaviors, including how they impact the plot and interact with other characters. Do you think that Nag and Nagaina are truly evil, or have they been unfairly cast as villains? Choose a side, and write a brief response explaining your position and analysis. Use several pieces of textual evidence to support your points.

Ready for Marcos

FICTION

Introduction

Twelve-year-old Monica Alvarez has a happy life. She is a star on the track team and has many good friends. But everything changes when her parents bring Marcos, her new baby brother, home from the hospital. Her parents want her to have more responsibilities. Monica wonders what it will mean to be a big sister. Is she ready? Is she willing?

8

VOCABULARY

8

vivacious
energetic and happy; lively

justify
to support with good reasons

covertly
done in secret

subtle
barely noticeable

Close Read & Skills Focus

6

After you have completed the First Read, you will be asked to go back and read the text more closely and critically. Before you begin your Close Read, you should read through the Skills Focus to get an idea of the concepts you will want to focus on during your second reading. You should work through the Skills Focus by making annotations, highlighting important concepts, and writing notes or questions in the "Notes" column. Depending on instructions from your teacher, you may need to respond online or use a separate piece of paper to start expanding on your thoughts and ideas.

Write

7

Your study of each selection will end with a writing assignment. For this assignment, you should use your notes, annotations, personal ideas, and answers to both the Think and Skills Focus questions. Be sure to read the prompt carefully and address each part of it in your writing.

English Language Learner

8

The English Language Learner texts focus on improving language proficiency. You will practice learning strategies and skills in individual and group activities to become better readers, writers, and speakers.

Extended Writing Project and Grammar

This is your opportunity to use genre characteristics and craft to compose meaningful, longer written works exploring the theme of each unit. You will draw information from your readings, research, and own life experiences to complete the assignment.

1 Writing Project

After you have read all of the unit text selections, you will move on to a writing project. Each project will guide you through the process of writing your essay. Student models will provide guidance and help you organize your thoughts. One unit ends with an **Extended Oral Project,** which will give you an opportunity to develop your oral language and communication skills.

2 Writing Process Steps

There are four steps in the writing process: Plan, Draft, Revise, and Edit and Publish. During each step, you will form and shape your writing project, and each lesson's peer review will give you the chance to receive feedback from your peers and teacher.

3 Writing Skills

Each Skill lesson focuses on a specific strategy or technique that you will use during your writing project. Each lesson presents a process for applying the skill to your own work and gives you the opportunity to practice it to improve your writing.

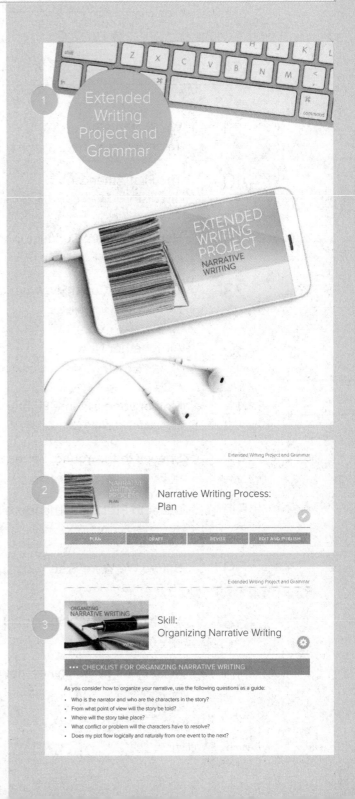

Chasing the Impossible

What makes a dream worth pursuing?

Genre Focus: ARGUMENTATIVE

Texts

 Paired Readings

Extended Writing Project and Grammar

Unit 3: Chasing the Impossible

What makes a dream worth pursuing?

JULIA ALVAREZ

Julia Alvarez (b. 1950) was born in New York City but spent the first ten years of her life living in the Dominican Republic. She attended Connecticut College before transferring to Middlebury College, where she received her bachelor's degree, and then earned a master's degree from Syracuse University. Her first published work was a collection of poetry, *The Homecoming* (1984), which was followed by her first novel, *How the Garcia Girls Lost Their Accents* (1991). She was awarded the National Medal of Arts in 2013 "for her extraordinary storytelling."

GWENDOLYN BROOKS

Pulitzer Prize-winning poet Gwendolyn Brooks (1917–2000) grew up in Chicago, Illinois, published her first poem at thirteen years old, and had written and published seventy-five poems by the age of sixteen. She was the first African American author to win the Pulitzer Prize, awarded for *Annie Allen* in 1950, a collection "devoted to small, carefully cerebrated, terse portraits of the Black urban poor" that chronicled life in the Bronzeville neighborhood of Chicago's South Side.

SAMPSON DAVIS, RAMECK HUNT, AND GEORGE JENKINS

Sampson Davis, Rameck Hunt, and George Jenkins (b. 1973) grew up in Newark, New Jersey, where they bonded over their shared interest in becoming medical professionals. They attended Seton Hall University together for their undergraduate degrees before moving on to medical school. Davis serves as an Emergency Medicine Physician; Hunt is a board-certified internist; Jenkins teaches as an assistant professor of clinical dentistry at Columbia University.

SHARON M. DRAPER

Sharon Mills Draper (b. 1948) was born in Cleveland, Ohio, and graduated from Pepperdine University. As an educator, she has been honored for her work by being invited to The White House on six different occasions. She's been named a National Teacher of the Year and holds three honorary doctorates. Draper is the author of two different *New York Times* Best Sellers, *Copper Sun* and *We Beat the Street*. She lives in Cincinnati.

MOTHER JONES

Mary G. Harris Jones (1837–1930), also known as Mother Jones, was born in Cork City, Ireland. Her family eventually immigrated to Canada, and Jones moved to the United States at the age of twenty-three and became a schoolteacher. In 1867, her husband and four children died during a yellow fever outbreak, and in 1871, she lost her home, shop, and all of her possessions in the Great Chicago Fire. Soon after, she joined the Knights of Labor and began organizing protests and strikes, advocating for children forced to work in Pennsylvania's silk mills.

BARBARA JORDAN

The first African American elected to the Texas Senate, and the first Southern African American woman to be elected to the United States House of Representatives, Barbara Jordan (1936–1996) was also the first woman to deliver a keynote address at a Democratic National Convention. Jordan helped lead impeachment proceedings against then-president Richard Nixon and was awarded the Presidential Medal of Freedom by President Bill Clinton in 1994. She was born in Houston, Texas, and attended Texas Southern University, where she was a national champion debater. She graduated from Boston University School of Law in 1959.

ANN PETRY

Born in Old Saybrook, Connecticut, Ann Petry (1908–1997) authored several books, including her 1946 bestseller *The Street,* which offered commentary on the problems facing African Americans in urban environments. The daughter of a pharmacist, she graduated from the Connecticut College of Pharmacy and worked at her family's drugstore. After getting married, she moved to New York City and began writing short stories for several African American journals, including *The Crisis* and *Opportunity*.

VIRGINIA HAMILTON

Raised in Yellow Springs, Ohio, as the youngest of five children, Virginia Hamilton (1934–2002) authored forty-one books, including *M.C. Higgins, the Great,* which received the National Book Award and the Newbery Medal. She moved to New York City in 1958, where she worked as a receptionist at a museum, as a nightclub singer, and at other odds jobs while she pursued her dream of being a writer. Hamilton's first book, *Zeely* (1967), won multiple awards, and in 1992 she received the Hans Christian Andersen Award for lifetime achievement in children's literature.

JUDITH PINKERTON JOSEPHSON

Judith Pinkerton Josephson is the author of several works, including *Mother Jones: Fierce Fighter for Workers' Rights, Allan Pinkerton: The Original Private Eye,* and *Growing Up in Pioneer America*. She's co-authored three other books and has taught all levels from preschool through junior high, in addition to facilitating seminars for adult writers. When she's not writing, she likes to play the violin, sing, sew, or knit.

DONOVAN LINCOLN

Dr. Don Lincoln (b. 1964) has spent over three decades "studying the most fundamental laws of nature." Lincoln works at Fermilab, the nation's particle physics and accelerator laboratory, where he's served as a senior scientist since 1999. He is also an adjunct professor of physics at the University of Notre Dame, and previously earned his PhD from Rice University in 1994. He is the author of over 1,000 scientific papers, has written magazine and online articles, and has published several books describing particle physics for non-scientists.

We Beat the Street

INFORMATIONAL TEXT
Sharon M. Draper, Sampson Davis,
Rameck Hunt, George Jenkins
2006

Introduction

studysync tv

Growing up in urban Newark, New Jersey, Rameck Hunt, Sampson Davis, and George Jenkins faced many challenges. Yet instead of accepting lives of gangs, drugs and prison, these childhood friends made a pact to overcome these obstacles and become doctors. In the following excerpt from their collective autobiography, *We Beat the Street*, Dr. George Jenkins shares one of his early influences—a teacher who gave him hope for the future.

"There was no doubt as to her power and authority in that classroom."

from Chapter 3: Isn't That School in the Ghetto?

1   **GEORGE, AGE 8** "Quit throwin' bottles in the street, man," eight-year-old George Jenkins yelled to his older brother, Garland.

2   "You can't make me," his brother taunted back. He picked up a green wine bottle he found in the gutter and tossed it onto the hard concrete of Muhammad Ali Avenue in Newark, New Jersey. It shattered into dozens of glistening fragments that shimmered in the sunlight.

3   "Suppose a car runs over the glass and gets a flat tire," George asked. Garland was almost ten, and George didn't think he acted his age.

4   "Too bad for them," Garland said as he tossed another bottle. "Hey, now, look at that one—two bounces and a smash!" He cheered as the brown beer bottle exploded and shattered.

5   "Hey, man, I'm outta here. I ain't gonna be late because of you." George glared at his brother before hurrying off in the direction of Louise A. Spencer Elementary School. Garland, he noticed, headed off in the other direction, once again skipping classes for the day.

6   George loved school. Even though it was located in what was described as the "inner city," it was relatively new and neat and clean. His third-grade teacher, Miss Viola Johnson, was a tiny ball of energy with a high-pitched voice and the same honey-colored skin as George's mother. There was no doubt as to her power and **authority** in that classroom. Miss Johnson made every day an adventure, and George hated to miss school, even on days when he was sick.

7   George slid quietly into the room, only a couple of minutes late, and grinned at Miss Johnson, who noticed his tardiness but said nothing.

8   "Today," she began, "we're going to continue talking about the writer named Shakespeare. How long ago did he live?" she asked the class.

9   "Four hundred years ago!" they responded immediately.

[handwritten margin notes: "George loves school" and "Garland"]

NOTES

10 "How many plays did he write?"

11 "Thirty-seven!"

Ms Johnson (handwritten)

12 George had no idea that Shakespeare was not usually taught in third grade. Miss Johnson simply offered it, and George, as well as the rest of his class, **absorbed** it.

13 "What was so cool about this Shakespeare dude, Miss Johnson?" a boy named Ritchie wanted to know. George wished he just would shut up so Miss Johnson could talk.

14 "Well, for one thing, Shakespeare wore an earring," Miss Johnson offered.

15 "For real? Real gold?" Ritchie seemed to be impressed.

16 "Here's another interesting fact," Miss Johnson said. "In order to seek his **fortune** as an actor and a writer, Shakespeare ran away from home shortly after he got married, leaving his wife and three children to make it without him," Miss Johnson explained.

17 "Sounds like yo' daddy!" Ritchie yelled to the boy sitting next to him. Both of them cracked up with laughter.

18 Every Tuesday she told them all about Shakespeare's time— about kings and castles, as well as about the rats and fleas that lived in the straw that most people used for bedding. "Did you know that during Shakespeare's time almost a third of the people who lived in London died one year from something called the Black Plague?" she asked the class.

19 "Why?" George asked.

20 "There were very few doctors at that time, and they didn't know what we know today about cleanliness and sanitation. Most people just threw their garbage out the window every morning, as well as the contents of their chamber pots. That's what they used at night. Toilets had not been invented yet."

21 "Yuk!" the class responded.

22 The class listened, fascinated and entranced with her stories, which taught them history, literature, math, and science without them even being aware of it. She passed out a children's version of *Hamlet,* full of pictures and explanations, and let them read the play and act out the fight scenes.

23 Every day went quickly in Miss Johnson's class, but she often stayed after school with them to make cookies or build projects. She even took them into New York City sometimes to let them see live plays on Broadway or to hear

Skill: Connotation and Denotation

Fascinated and entranced have similar definitions. Both mean "to be very interested." The connotations of these words are positive. They make me realize how much George loves school and how amazing his teacher is.

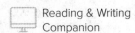

Reading & Writing Companion

orchestra concerts at Lincoln Center. George loved to listen to the drums and horns and violins as they mixed up together in that huge concert hall.

24. When her students formed the Shakespeare Club, Miss Johnson even helped them get sweaters. They were deep burgundy with the name of the club embroidered on the pocket. George and his classmates wore them proudly to a concert one afternoon.

25. During the intermission,[1] a woman wearing too much perfume and a mink[2] coat, even though it was the middle of spring, walked up to George and said, "What lovely sweaters you and your classmates are wearing."

26. "Thank you, ma'am," George said with a grin, touching the careful embroidery.

27. "What private school do you children attend?" the woman asked.

28. Miss Johnson walked over to the woman and said proudly, "These are students from Louise Spencer Elementary, a public school in the Central Ward."

29. "But they're so well behaved," the woman said with surprise. "Isn't that school in the ghetto?"

30. Miss Johnson gave the woman a look that could have melted that mink coat and led her students away. George looked back at the woman with hurt and confusion. He wished he could have tripped the smelly old lady.

31. On the way back home from this trip, George, always the quiet kid, sat alone on the bus seat. "Mind if I sit next to you, George?" someone asked.

32. He looked up, pulled his long legs out of the aisle, and smiled at her. "Sure, Miss Johnson."

33. "Did that woman upset you?" she asked. George shrugged.

34. "I don't know. She smelled like mothballs."

35. "There will always be people like that, you know," Miss Johnson explained.

36. "Yeah, I know."

37. "And you can either let them hold you back, or you can ignore them and go on and do your thing."

38. "Yeah, I know." George didn't want to admit how much the woman's words had hurt. He changed the subject. "That was a good concert, Miss Johnson. I think it's really cool that you take us to stuff like this."

---

1. **intermission** a short break in the middle of a film, play, or performance
2. **mink** a small carnivorous mammal slaughtered for its fur

39   "Perhaps when you go to college you can learn to write symphonies or plays of your own," she said.

40   "College? I never even thought about it." To George, the idea of college seemed like something foreign and **vague,** like going to China or the moon.

41   "Of course you'll go to college. You're one of the smartest children in my class." Miss Johnson spoke with certainty. "I have high hopes and great expectations for you, George."

42   "Maybe you do, but some kids think it ain't cool to be too smart, you know," George told her.

43   "That's the dumbest thing I ever heard!" Miss Johnson said loudly. The other kids on the bus looked up to see what had upset her.

44   "You don't understand," George said quietly. "It's hard to fit in with your boys if your grades are too good."

45   "Nonsense!" Miss Johnson replied. "You don't really believe that."

46   George grinned at her. "Yeah, I guess you're right. I guess I really don't care what they think of me."

47   "College is cool, George. If you can fit in there, you've got it made."

48   "Doesn't it take a long time?" George asked, chewing on his lip. He felt a combination of excitement and wonder.

Skill: Connotation and Denotation

*There is a lot of emotion here.
Boarded-up means "covered," and defeated means "to lose badly." Both have negative feelings.
George describes his neighborhood with these words. He must be upset or confused after his experience at the theater. This phrase also lets me know that George lives in a poor area of town.*

49   "It takes four years to complete the first part of college," she explained. "At the end of that time, you'll be four years older whether you go to college or not, so you might as well go and get as much knowledge in your head as you can."

50   George looked out of the bus window and thought about what she had said. As the field-trip bus got closer to his neighborhood in Newark, he looked at the tall, poverty-ridden, high-rise apartments like the one he lived in; the boarded-up and defeated stores; and the trash all over the streets.

51   "I don't know how," he said quietly, helpless in his lack of knowledge.

52   Miss Johnson didn't laugh, however. She just smiled and said, "It's not very hard. Just do your best, keep your nose out of trouble, and one day the doors will open for you."

53   For the first time, George could see a **glimpse** of light, a spark of hope and possibility. College. What a cool idea.

Excerpted from *We Beat the Street* by Sampson Davis, reprinted by Puffin Books.

WE BEAT THE STREET
studysync®

First Read

Read *We Beat the Street*. After you read, complete the Think Questions below.

☁ THINK QUESTIONS

1. Write two or three sentences explaining how George feels about school.

2. Why do the students think Miss Johnson is a good teacher? Cite specific examples from the text.

3. What goal does Miss Johnson inspire George to set for himself? Explain, including evidence from the text in your answer.

4. Read the following dictionary entry:

    absorb

    ab•sorb \ əb'zôrb \ *verb*

    a. to soak up by physical or chemical action
    b. to take in information or knowledge
    c. to reduce the intensity of a sound
    d. to engross or capture someone's attention

    Which definition most closely matches the meaning of **absorbed** as it is used in paragraph 12? Write the correct definition of *absorbed* here and explain how you figured out the correct meaning.

5. Use context clues to determine the meaning of **fortune** as it is used in paragraph 16 of *We Beat the Street*. Write your definition here and identify clues that helped you figure out the meaning.

Skill:
Connotation and Denotation

Use the Checklist to analyze Connotation and Denotation in *We Beat the Street*. Refer to the sample student annotations about Connotation and Denotation in the text.

••• CHECKLIST FOR CONNOTATION AND DENOTATION

In order to identify the connotative meanings of words and phrases, use the following steps:

✓ First, note unfamiliar words and phrases; key words used to describe important individuals, events, and ideas; or words that inspire an emotional reaction.

✓ Next, determine and note the denotative meaning of words by consulting reference materials such as a dictionary, a glossary, or a thesaurus.

To better understand the meanings of words and phrases as they are used in a text, including connotative meanings, use the following questions:

✓ What is the genre or subject of the text? How does that affect the possible meaning of a word or phrase?

✓ Does the word create a positive, negative, or neutral emotion?

✓ What synonyms or alternative phrasing help you describe the connotative meaning of the word?

Skill:
Connotation and Denotation

Reread paragraphs 41–48 of *We Beat the Street*. Then, using the Checklist on the previous page, answer the multiple-choice questions below.

⟳ YOUR TURN

1. This question has two parts. First, answer Part A. Then, answer Part B.

   Part A: Which answer best describes the connotation of the word *boys* as it is used in paragraph 44?

   ○ A. young men

   ○ B. friends

   ○ C. brothers

   ○ D. bullies

   Part B: Which line from the passage supports your answer to Part A?

   ○ A. "I have high hopes and great expectations for you, George."

   ○ B. "Nonsense!" Miss Johnson replied. "You don't really believe that."

   ○ C. " . . . some kids think it ain't cool to be too smart, you know."

   ○ D. "You don't understand," George said quietly.

2. This question has two parts. First, answer Part A. Then, answer Part B.

   Part A: Which answer best describes the connotation of the phrase *chewing on his lip* as it is used in paragraph 48?

   - ○ A. thoughtful
   - ○ B. angry
   - ○ C. happy
   - ○ D. tense

   Part B: Which line from the passage supports your answer to Part A?

   - ○ A. "I have high hopes and great expectations for you, George."
   - ○ B. "Doesn't it take a long time?" George asked
   - ○ C. George grinned at her. "Yeah, I guess you're right."
   - ○ D. "College is cool, George."

WE BEAT THE STREET
study sync

Close Read

Reread *We Beat the Street*. As you reread, complete the Skills Focus questions below. Then use your answers and annotations from the questions to help you complete the Write activity.

◎ SKILLS FOCUS

1. Identify words or phrases that have positive connotations. Write a note about how those words are used to impact the meaning or your understanding of the text.

2. What main or central ideas are developed about George, the field trip, or school? Highlight evidence from the beginning and end of the story. Then, write notes describing how the evidence develops the main or central ideas.

3. In paragraph 40, George says, "College? I never even thought about it." Identify details about George's neighborhood that may have prevented George from understanding that college was an option.

4. This excerpt from *We Beat the Street* describes the real experiences from the childhood of George Jenkins, who went on to become a doctor. Identify textual evidence that shows Jenkins's purpose in providing this information to readers.

5. Identify examples of how Miss Johnson helps her students to "dream impossible dreams" in the excerpt from *We Beat the Street*.

✎ WRITE

LITERARY ANALYSIS: In this excerpt from his autobiography, Dr. George Jenkins shares the true story of one of his early influences—a teacher who gave him hope for the future. How did the experiences described in the excerpt affect Jenkins? How does Jenkins's use of words with strong connotations help you better understand the experiences? What impact does his word choice have on readers? Write a response answering these questions using evidence from the text.

Please note that excerpts and passages in the StudySync® library and this workbook are intended as touchstones to generate interest in an author's work. The excerpts and passages do not substitute for the reading of entire texts, and StudySync® strongly recommends that students seek out and purchase the whole literary or informational work in order to experience it as the author intended. Links to online resellers are available in our digital library. In addition, complete works may be ordered through an authorized reseller by filling out and returning to StudySync® the order form enclosed in this workbook.

Reading & Writing
Companion

9

The First Americans

ARGUMENTATIVE TEXT
The Grand Council Fire
of American Indians
1927

Introduction

In 1927, Chicago Mayor William Hale Thompson won re-election with the campaign slogan "America First." One of the issues Thompson campaigned on was that American history textbooks had been biased in favor of the British, ignoring the contributions of other immigrant groups, such as the Irish and Germans. Members of the Grand Council Fire of American Indians took issue with Hale's push to revise textbooks to be "100-percent American," writing a public letter to the mayor to demonstrate the ways in which American history had unjustly treated American

"We ask only that our story be told in fairness."

December 1, 1927

To the mayor of Chicago:—

1   You tell all white men "America First." We believe in that. We are the only ones, truly, that are 100 percent. We therefore ask you while you are teaching school children about America First, teach them truth about the First Americans.

Skill: Language, Style, and Audience

2   We do not know if school histories are pro-British, but we do know that they are unjust to the life of our people—the American Indian. They call all white victories, battles, and all Indian victories, massacres. The battle with Custer[1] has been taught to school children as a fearful massacre on our part. We ask that this, as well as other **incidents,** be told fairly. If the Custer battle was a massacre, what was Wounded Knee[2]?

3   History books teach that Indians were murderers—is it murder to fight in self-defense? Indians killed white men because white men took their lands, ruined their hunting grounds, burned their forests, destroyed their buffalo. White men penned our people on **reservations**, then took away the reservations. White men who rise to protect their property are called **patriots**—Indians who do the same are called murderers.

The authors use the word murderers *several times in this paragraph. They point out that white men are called patriots when they protect their property while Native Americans are called murderers. The authors are clearly expressing their anger at this unfairness. They demand action.*

4   White men call Indians **treacherous**—but no mention is made of broken treaties on the part of the white man. White men say that Indians were always fighting. It was only our lack of skill in white man's warfare that led to our defeat. An Indian mother prayed that her boy be a great medicine man[3] rather than a great warrior. It is true that we had our own small battles, but in the main we were peace-loving and home-loving.

5   White men called Indians thieves—and yet we lived in frail skin lodges and needed no locks or iron bars. White men call Indians savages. What is

---

1. **Custer** General George Armstrong Custer (1839–1876) was the leader of U.S. troops killed at the Battle of the Little Bighorn.
2. **Wounded Knee** the massacre of Lakota people that took place at Wounded Knee Creek, South Dakota, on December 29, 1890
3. **medicine man** a ceremonial priest or doctor of Native Americans

**Skill:
Summarizing**

Who? Grand Council
What? says Indians are
peaceful and civilized
Where? in America
When? now and in the
past Why and How?
art, no locks

**Skill: Language,
Style, and
Audience**

In this paragraph, the
authors establish a
more formal and
positive tone. They use
"brilliant oratory" to
formally describe the
elegant speeches made
by their statesmen and
to show their knowledge
as equal of that of
white men. This word
choice shows that the
Native Americans are
proud of their history.

civilization? Its marks are a noble religion and philosophy, original arts, stirring music, rich history and legend. We had these. Then we were not savages, but a civilized race.

6   We made blankets that were beautiful that the white man with all his machinery has never been able to duplicate. We made baskets that were beautiful. We wove in beads and colored quills, designs that were not just decorative motifs, but were the outward **expression** of our very thoughts. We made pottery—pottery that was useful and beautiful as well. Why not make school children acquainted with the beautiful handicrafts in which we were skilled? Put in every school Indian blankets, baskets, pottery.

7   We sang songs that carried in their melodies all the sounds of nature—the running of waters, the sighing of winds, and the calls of the animals. Teach these to your children that they may come to love nature as we love it.

8   We had our statesmen—and their oratory has never been equalled. Teach the children some of these speeches of our people, remarkable for their brilliant oratory. We played games—games that brought good health and sound bodies. Why not put these in your schools? We told stories. Why not teach school children more of the wholesome proverbs and legends of our people? Tell them how we loved all that was beautiful. That we killed game only for food, not for fun. Indians think white men who kill for fun are murderers.

9   Tell your children of the friendly acts of Indians to the white people who first settled here. Tell them of our leaders and heroes and their deeds. Tell them of Indians such as Black Partridge,[4] Shabbona[5] and others who many times saved the people of Chicago at great danger to themselves. Put in your history books the Indian's part in the World War. Tell how the Indian fought for a country of which he was not a citizen, for a flag to which he had no claim, and for a people that have treated him unjustly.

10   The Indian has long been hurt by these unfair books. We ask only that our story be told in fairness. We do not ask you to overlook what we did, but we do ask you to understand it. A true program of America First will give a generous place to the culture and history of the American Indian.

11   We ask this, Chief, to keep sacred the memory of our people.

---

4. **Black Partridge** an early 19th-century Potawatomi chief who defended settlers at the Battle of Fort Dearborn and signed a treaty with the U.S.
5. **Shabbona** a 19th-century Ottawa/Potawatomi chief who switched sides to the U.S. in the War of 1812

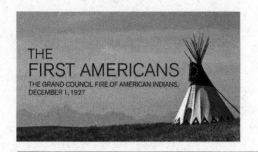

First Read

Read "The First Americans." After you read, complete the Think Questions below.

Copyright © BookheadEd Learning, LLC

☁ THINK QUESTIONS

1. According to the letter, what do American history books teach students about Native Americans?

2. According to the letter, what do history books teach students about white men? Cite specific examples mentioned in the letter.

3. What positive examples of Native American culture does the letter discuss?

4. Read the following dictionary entry:

   reservation

   res•er•va•tion \rez'-ər-vā'-shən\ *noun*
   a. public land set aside for special use
   b. a guaranteed place at a restaurant or hotel
   c. a misgiving or doubt

   Which definition most closely matches the meaning of **reservation** as it is used in paragraph 3? Write the correct definition of *reservation* here and explain how you figured out the correct meaning.

5. What is the meaning of the word **expression** as it is used in paragraph 6? Write the definition of *expression* and explain how you figured out the correct meaning.

Skill:
Summarizing

Use the Checklist to analyze Summarizing in "The First Americans." Refer to the sample student annotations about Summarizing in the text.

••• CHECKLIST FOR SUMMARIZING

In order to determine how to write an objective summary of an informational text or other nonfiction texts, note the following:

- ✓ informational text elements, such as individuals, events, or ideas

- ✓ the details that readers must know in order to understand the main idea(s)

- ✓ answers to the basic questions *who, what, where, when, why,* and *how*

- ✓ stay objective, and do not add your own personal thoughts, judgments, or opinions to the summary

To provide an objective summary of an informational text or other nonfiction texts, consider the following questions:

- ✓ Which details develop the main idea(s)?

- ✓ What are the answers to basic *who, what, where, when, why,* and *how* questions?

- ✓ In what order should I put the most important details to make my summary logical?

- ✓ How can I briefly state the most important details in my own words?

- ✓ Is my summary objective, or have I added my own thoughts, judgments, or personal opinions?

Skill:
Summarizing

Reread paragraphs 6–7 of "The First Americans." Then, using the Checklist on the previous page, answer the multiple-choice questions below.

↻ YOUR TURN

1. Which of the following details from paragraph 6 most clearly supports the main idea of the paragraph?

   ○ A. ". . . white man with all his machinery has never been able to duplicate."

   ○ B. ". . . the outward expression of our very thoughts."

   ○ C. "We made pottery—pottery that was useful and beautiful as well."

   ○ D. "Put in every school Indian blankets, baskets, pottery."

2. What is the best objective summary of paragraph 6?

   ○ A. Native Americans are better than white men at making blankets.

   ○ B. American school children should be given the chance to study the art of Native American handicrafts.

   ○ C. Blankets, pottery, and other arts made by Native Americans are just as good as or better than those made by white artists.

   ○ D. School children in America are taught that white artists make better art than Native American artists.

3. What is the best objective summary of paragraph 7?

   ○ A. The songs sung by Native Americans were absolutely amazing and should be taught in school.

   ○ B. Native American songs reflect the sounds of nature, including the calls of wild animals.

   ○ C. Students can learn to love nature by studying Native American songs, which celebrate nature.

   ○ D. Singing songs about nature is a good way to learn about the natural world.

Skill: Language, Style, and Audience

Use the Checklist to analyze Language, Style, and Audience in "The First Americans." Refer to the sample student annotations about Language, Style, and Audience in the text.

••• CHECKLIST FOR LANGUAGE, STYLE, AND AUDIENCE

In order to determine an author's style, do the following:

- ✓ identify and define any unfamiliar words or phrases

- ✓ use context, including the meaning of surrounding words and phrases

- ✓ note possible reactions to the author's word choice

- ✓ examine your reaction to the author's word choice and how the author's choice affected your reaction

To analyze the impact of specific word choice on meaning and tone, ask the following questions:

- ✓ How did your understanding of the language change during your analysis?

- ✓ What stylistic choices can you identify in the text? How does the style influence your understanding of the language?

- ✓ How could various audiences interpret this language? What different possible emotional responses can you list?

- ✓ How does the writer's choice of words impact or create a specific tone in the text?

Skill: Language, Style, and Audience

Reread paragraphs 4–7 of "The First Americans." Then, using the Checklist on the previous page, answer the multiple-choice questions below.

⟳ YOUR TURN

1. In paragraph 4, the use of the word **treacherous** establishes what feeling?

   ○ A. fury
   ○ B. depression
   ○ C. loneliness
   ○ D. elation

2. How does the use of the word **treacherous** contribute to the tone of this part of the letter?

   ○ A. The word *treacherous* shows the sadness the Native American chiefs feel about their own history.
   ○ B. The word *treacherous* shows the dangerous lifestyle of Native Americans and white men.
   ○ C. The word *treacherous* shows the peaceful ways of the Native Americans.
   ○ D. The word *treacherous* shows the anger the Native American chiefs feel about their unfair treatment by white men and the fury they feel about their misrepresentation in history.

3. In paragraph 6, what do the writers mean by "were the outward expression of our very thoughts"?

   ○ A. The angry thoughts the Native Americans have toward the white men
   ○ B. The clothing that Native Americans wear
   ○ C. The beautiful crafts the Native Americans have made from their imagination
   ○ D. The letters Native Americans have written to show their thoughts

4. What is the tone of paragraphs 6 and 7?

   ○ A. formal and proud
   ○ B. sad and bitter
   ○ C. informal and angry
   ○ D. satisfied and thankful

Please note that excerpts and passages in the StudySync® library and this workbook are intended as touchstones to generate interest in an author's work. The excerpts and passages do not substitute for the reading of entire texts, and StudySync® strongly recommends that students seek out and purchase the whole literary or informational work in order to experience it as the author intended. Links to online resellers are available in our digital library. In addition, complete works may be ordered through an authorized reseller by filling out and returning to StudySync® the order form enclosed in this workbook.

Reading & Writing Companion   17

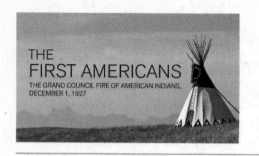

THE
FIRST AMERICANS
THE GRAND COUNCIL FIRE OF AMERICAN INDIANS,
DECEMBER 1, 1927

Close Read

Reread "The First Americans." As you reread, complete the Skills Focus questions below. Then use your answers and annotations from the questions to help you complete the Write activity.

◎ SKILLS FOCUS

1. Identify passages that show the purpose of the letter "The First Americans." Explain what you think motivated the members of the Council to write this letter.

2. Identify examples in the letter of how history books in the 1920s portrayed Native Americans. Summarize how Native Americans were portrayed in textbooks.

3. Identify examples of emotional word choice throughout the letter. Explain the effect of this language on the style of the letter.

4. **Style** is the distinctive use of language to achieve the purpose of the writer. Identify words or phrases that the authors use to create a knowledgeable, formal style. Explain how these formal words or phrases might affect the reader.

5. An ideal version of something is sometimes called a "dream" version. Identify a passage in the text that shows what a "dream" U.S. history textbook would have been for the Grand Council. Explain how the textual evidence supports your ideas.

✏ WRITE

LITERARY ANALYSIS: Objectively summarize the main points of the letter. Then explain how the Grand Council's language and style help to clarify and emphasize the main points. How does their word choice affect the tone or style of the letter? Use evidence from the text to support your analysis.

Harriet Tubman:
Conductor on the Underground Railroad

INFORMATIONAL TEXT
Ann Petry
1955

Introduction

The years prior to the Civil War were especially perilous for once-enslaved people who had escaped, but Harriet Tubman returned again and again to the South to help fugitives gain freedom. Where did her physical and moral courage come from? This excerpt from a biography of Tubman by Ann Petry (1908–1997) describes how six-year-old Harriet learned about life on the plantation and came to understand the bitter truths about slavery.

"There was something free and wild in Harriet . . ."

excerpt from Chapter Three: Six Years Old

1   By the time Harriet Ross was six years old, she had **unconsciously absorbed** many kinds of knowledge, almost with the air she breathed. She could not, for example, have said how or at what moment she learned that she was a slave.

2   She knew that her brothers and sisters, her father and mother, and all the other people who lived in the quarter,[1] men, women and children, were slaves.

Frederick Douglass and Harriet Tubman, two of the best-known African Americans of the Civil War era, were both enslaved in Maryland. Both became leaders in the American abolitionist movement, helping to end slavery in the United States.

3   She had been taught to say, "Yes, Missus," "No, Missus," to white women, "Yes, Mas'r," "No, Mas'r," to white men. Or, "Yes, sah," "No, sah."

4   At the same time, someone had taught her where to look for the North Star, the star that stayed **constant,** not rising in the east and setting in the west as the other stars appeared to do; and told her that anyone walking toward the North could use that star as a guide.

5   She knew about fear, too. Sometimes at night, or during the day, she heard the furious galloping of horses, not just one horse, several horses, thud of the hoofbeats along the road, jingle of harness. She saw the grown folks freeze into stillness, not moving, scarcely breathing, while they listened. She could not remember who first told her that those furious hoofbeats meant the patrollers were going past, in pursuit of a runaway. Only the slaves said patterollers,[2] whispering the word.

---

1. **quarter** rooms or lodging
2. **patterollers** gangs of white men who disciplined enslaved people at night

6   Old Rit would say a prayer that the hoofbeats would not stop. If they did, there would be the dreadful sound of screams. Because the runaway slave had been caught, would be whipped, and finally sold to the chain gang.[3]

7   Thus Harriet already shared the uneasiness and the fear of the grownups. But she shared their pleasures, too. She knew moments of pride when the overseer consulted Ben, her father, about the weather. Ben could tell if it was going to rain, when the first frost would come, tell whether there was going to be a long stretch of clear sunny days. Everyone on the plantation admired this skill of Ben's. Even the master, Edward Brodas.

8   The other slaves were in awe of Ben because he could prophesy[4] about the weather. Harriet stood close to him when he studied the sky, licked his forefinger and held it up to determine the direction of the wind, then announced that there would be rain or frost or fair weather.

9   There was something free and wild in Harriet because of Ben. He talked about the arrival of the wild ducks, the thickness of the winter coat of muskrats and of rabbits. He was always talking about the woods, the berries that grew there, the strange haunting cries of some of the birds, the loud sound their wings made when they were disturbed and flew up suddenly. He spoke of the way the owls flew, their feathers so soft that they seemed to glide, soundless, through the air.

10   Ben knew about rivers and creeks and swampy places. He said that the salt water from the Bay reached into the rivers and streams for long distances. You could stick your finger in the river water and lick it and you could taste the salt from the Bay.

11   He had been all the way to the Chesapeake. He had seen storms there. He said the Big Buckwater River, which lay off to the southeast of the plantation, was just a little stream compared to the Choptank, and the Choptank was less than nothing compared to the Bay.

12   All through the plantation, from the Big House to the stables, to the fields, he had a reputation for **absolute** honesty. He had never been known to tell a lie. He was a valued worker and a trusted one.

13   Ben could tell wonderful stories, too. So could her mother, Old Rit, though Rit's were mostly from the Bible. Rit told about Moses and the children of Israel, about how the sea parted so that the children walked across on dry land, about the plague of locusts, about how some of the children were afraid on the long journey to the Promised Land, and so cried out: "It had been better for us to serve the Egyptians, than that we should die in the wilderness."

---

3. **chain gang** a group of men involuntarily chained together for work
4. **prophesy** to have a vision of the future; to predict

14 Old Rit taught Harriet the words of that song that the slaves were forbidden to sing, because of the man named Denmark Vesey, who had urged the other slaves to revolt by telling them about Moses and the children of Israel. Sometimes, in the quarter, Harriet heard snatches of it, sung under the breath, almost whispered: "Go down, Moses . . ." But she learned the words so well that she never forgot them.

15 She was aware of all these things and many other things too. She learned to separate the days of the week. Sunday was a special day. There was no work in the fields. The slaves cooked in the quarter and washed their clothes and sang and told stories.

16 There was another special day, issue day, which occurred at the end of the month. It was the day that food and clothes were issued to the slaves. One of the slaves was sent to the Big House, with a wagon, to bring back the monthly allowance of food. Each slave received eight pounds of pickled pork or its **equivalent** in fish, one bushel of Indian meal (corn meal), one pint of salt.

17 Once a year, on issue day, they received clothing. The men were given two tow-linen shirts, two pairs of trousers, one of tow-linen, the other woolen, and a woolen jacket for winter. The grownups received one pair of yarn stockings and a pair of shoes.

18 The children under eight had neither shoes, stockings, jacket nor trousers. They were issued two tow-linen shirts a year—short, one-piece garments made of a coarse material like burlap, reaching to the knees. These shirts were worn night and day. They were changed once a week. When they were worn out, the children went naked until the next allowance day.

19 Men and women received a coarse blanket apiece. The children kept warm as best they could.

Excerpted from *Harriet Tubman: Conductor on the Underground Railroad* by Ann Petry, published by Amistad Press.

✏ WRITE

NARRATIVE: Write a story of approximately 300 words about a typical day in Harriet Tubman's life when she was six years old. Generate ideas for your narrative, using these questions: What events might have taken place? What might she have done, heard, seen, and thought about? Base your narrative on details in this passage.

The People Could Fly:
American Black Folktales

FICTION
Virginia Hamilton
1985

Introduction

Virginia Hamilton (1936–2002) was a children's book author who retold African American folklore with humor, magic, and mystery in her collection *The People Could Fly: American Black Folktales*. In this excerpt from the titular folktale, you'll learn about why enslaved West Africans took off their wings

"They say the people could fly. Say that long ago in Africa, some of the people knew magic."

1   They say the people could fly. Say that long ago in Africa, some of the people knew magic. And they would walk upon the air like climbin' up on a gate. And they flew like blackbirds over the fields. Black, shiny wings flappin' against the blue up there.

2   Then, many of the people were captured for Slavery. The ones that could fly shed their wings. They couldn't take their wings across the water on slave ships. Too crowded, don't you know.

3   The folks were full of **misery,** then. Got sick with the up and down of the sea. So they forgot about flyin' when they could no longer breathe the sweet scent of Africa.

4   Say the people who could fly kept their power, although they shed their wings. They looked the same as the other people from Africa who had been coming over, who had dark skin. Say you couldn't tell anymore one who could fly from one who couldn't.

5   One such who could was an old man, call him Toby. And standin' tall, yet afraid, was a young woman who once had wings. Call her Sarah. Now Sarah carried a babe tied to her back. She **trembled** to be so hard worked and scorned.

6   The slaves **labored** in the fields from sunup to sundown. The owner of the slaves callin' himself their Master. Say he was a hard lump of clay. A hard, glinty coal. A hard rock pile, wouldn't be moved. His Overseer[1] on horseback pointed out the slaves who were slowin' down. So the one called Driver[2] cracked his whip over the slow ones to make them move faster. That whip was a slice-open cut of pain. So they did move faster. Had to.

7   Sarah hoed and chopped the row as the babe on her back slept.

8   Say the child grew hungry. That babe started up **bawling** too loud. Sarah couldn't stop to feed it. Couldn't stop to **soothe** and quiet it down. She let it cry. She didn't want to. She had no heart to **croon** to it.

---

1. **Overseer** a plantation employee in charge of enslaved people
2. **Driver** a deputy of an overseer who kept enslaved people working hard through threats, injury, or intimidation

9 "Keep that thing quiet," called the Overseer. He pointed his finger at the babe. The woman scrunched low. The Driver cracked his whip across the babe anyhow. The babe hollered like any hurt child, and the woman fell to the earth.

10 The old man that was there, Toby, came and helped her to her feet.

11 "I must go soon," she told him.

12 "Soon," he said.

13 Sarah couldn't stand up straight any longer. She was too weak. The sun burned her face. The babe cried and cried, "Pity me, oh, pity me," say it sounded like. Sarah was so sad and starving, she sat down in the row.

14 "Get up, you black cow," called the Overseer. He pointed his hand and the Driver's whip snarled around Sarah's legs. Her sack dress tore into rags. Her legs bled onto the earth. She couldn't get up.

15 Toby was there where there was no one to help her and the babe.

16 "Now, before it's too late," panted Sarah. "Now, Father!"

17 "Yes, Daughter, the time is come," Toby answered. "Go as you know how to go!"

18 He raised his arms, holding them out to her. "*Kum...yali, kum buba tambe*," and more magic words, said so quickly; they sounded like whispers and sighs.

19 The young woman lifted one foot on the air. Then the other. She flew clumsily at first, with the child now held tightly in her arms. Then she felt the magic, the African mystery. Say she rose just as free as a bird. As light as a feather.

20 The Overseer rode after her, hollerin'. Sarah flew over the fences. She flew over the woods. Tall trees could not snag her. Nor could the Overseer. She flew like an eagle now, until she was gone from sight. No one dared speak about it. Couldn't believe it. But it was, because they that was there saw that it was.

Excerpted from *The People Could Fly: American Black Folktales* by Virginia Hamilton, published by Alfred A. Knopf.

First Read

Read "The People Could Fly." After you read, complete the Think Questions below.

☁ THINK QUESTIONS

1. Why did the people lose their wings? Cite textual evidence from the first two paragraphs to explain your answer.

2. Why does Sarah need to leave the plantation? Use ideas that are directly stated in the text and ideas you have inferred from clues in the selection. Support your inferences with textual evidence.

3. Why is Sarah able to fly without wings at the end of the folktale? Refer to one or more details that are directly stated as well as inferences drawn from the text.

4. Find the word **soothe** in paragraph 8 of "The People Could Fly." Use context clues in the surrounding sentences, as well as the sentence in which the word appears, to determine the word's meaning. Write your definition here and identify clues that helped you figure out the meaning.

5. Use context clues to determine the meaning of the word **labored** as it is used in paragraph 6 of "The People Could Fly." Write your definition and identify clues that helped you figure out the meaning. Then check the meaning in a dictionary.

Skill:
Compare and Contrast

Use the Checklist to analyze Compare and Contrast in "The People Could Fly."

••• CHECKLIST FOR COMPARE AND CONTRAST

In order to compare and contrast texts within and across different forms and genres, do the following:

✓ choose two or more texts with similar subjects, topics, settings or characters

✓ highlight evidence that reveals each text's theme or central message

- consider what happens as a result of the characters' words and actions

- note ways in which the texts are similar and different

To compare and contrast texts within and across different forms or genres, consider the following questions:

✓ What are the similarities and differences in the subjects or topics of the texts I have chosen?

✓ Have I looked at the words of each character, as well as what the characters do, to help me determine the theme of each work?

Please note that excerpts and passages in the StudySync® library and this workbook are intended as touchstones to generate interest in an author's work. The excerpts and passages do not substitute for the reading of entire texts, and StudySync® strongly recommends that students seek out and purchase the whole literary or informational work in order to experience it as the author intended. Links to online resellers are available in our digital library. In addition, complete works may be ordered through an authorized reseller by filling out and returning to StudySync® the order form enclosed in this workbook.

Reading & Writing
Companion

27

Skill:
Compare and Contrast

Reread paragraphs 18–19 of the "The People Could Fly" and paragraph 13 of *Harriet Tubman: Conductor on the Underground Railroad*. Match the observations to the appropriate selection in the chart below.

YOUR TURN

	Observations
A	Both use figurative language to talk about escaping.
B	Both are about people escaping from oppression.
C	The story about fleeing Israelites represents the enslaved people trying to escape from their oppressors.
D	The enslaved people tell stories about Biblical escapes.
E	Sarah is described as a bird when she escapes.
F	Sarah flies away using magic and help from her friend.

Harriet Tubman	Both	The People Could Fly

Close Read

Reread "The People Could Fly." As you reread, complete the Skills Focus questions below. Then use your answers and annotations from the questions to help you complete the Write activity.

◎ SKILLS FOCUS

1. Both "The People Could Fly" and *Harriet Tubman: Conductor on the Underground Railroad* talk about how secret knowledge empowers enslaved people. Identify evidence where enslaved people have secret knowledge that helps them. Write a note comparing the use of secret knowledge in "The People Could Fly" to the use of secret knowledge in *Harriet Tubman*.

2. Find times in the two stories when enslaved children are afraid. Make annotations to explain how "The People Could Fly" uses the historical facts to show how slavery created a culture of fear.

3. In paragraph 9 of *Harriet Tubman: Conductor on the Underground Railroad*, the author describes Ben's connection to nature by referencing a number of birds—for example, ducks and owls.

Highlight evidence from "The People Could Fly" that refers to birds. Make annotations to explain how the folktale uses bird imagery in comparison to the imagery in *Harriet Tubman*.

4. Find words with connotative meanings that add to the meaning of "The People Could Fly." Write a note to explain how the connotations express the relationship between Toby and Sarah.

5. Both texts focus on the enslavement and mistreatment of enslaved people during the most tragic period in American history. Find details that help you understand how these circumstances led to pursuing dreams in dangerous times, and make notes about how the characters pursue their dreams and what stands in the way.

✎ WRITE

COMPARE AND CONTRAST: *Harriet Tubman: Conductor on the Underground Railroad* and "The People Could Fly" are about similar topics but in different genres. The first is a historical account of slavery in American history. The second is a fictional portrayal of the same topic or theme. How did Virginia Hamilton use historical facts in "The People Could Fly"? What changes does she make and what are the effects? Remember to support your analysis with evidence from the texts.

Please note that excerpts and passages in the StudySync® library and this workbook are intended as touchstones to generate interest in an author's work. The excerpts and passages do not substitute for the reading of entire texts, and StudySync® strongly recommends that students seek out and purchase the whole literary or informational work in order to experience it as the author intended. Links to online resellers are available in our digital library. In addition, complete works may be ordered through an authorized reseller by filling out and returning to StudySync® the order form enclosed in this workbook.

Reading & Writing Companion   29

All Together Now

ARGUMENTATIVE TEXT
Barbara Jordan
1976

Introduction

I n 1966, Barbara Jordan (1936–1996) became the first African American woman elected to the Texas State Senate. She later became the first African American woman to represent a southern state in Congress when she was elected to the U.S. House of Representatives in 1972. Jordan worked hard to improve the lives of people in her district, sponsored bills that increased workers' wages, and fought for women's rights. She was considered a gifted public speaker and was selected to give the keynote speech at the 1976 Democratic National Convention in New York. Her highly acclaimed speech is excerpted here.

"For the American idea, though it is shared by all of us, is realized in each one of us."

1 Thank you ladies and gentlemen for a very warm reception.

2 It was one hundred and forty-four years ago that members of the Democratic Party first met in convention to select a Presidential candidate. Since that time, Democrats have continued to convene once every four years and draft a party platform[1] and nominate a Presidential candidate. And our meeting this week is a continuation of that tradition. But there is something different about tonight. There is something special about tonight. What is different? What is special?

Congresswoman Barbara Jordan was the first African American woman to give the keynote speech at the Democratic National Convention.

3 I, Barbara Jordan, am a keynote speaker.[2]

4 A lot of years passed since 1832, and during that time it would have been most unusual for any national political party to ask a Barbara Jordan to deliver a keynote address. But tonight, here I am. And I feel that notwithstanding the past that my presence here is one additional bit of evidence that the American Dream need not forever be **deferred**.

5 Now that I have this grand **distinction**, what in the world am I supposed to say? . . . I could list the many problems which Americans have. I could list the problems which cause people to feel cynical, angry, frustrated: problems which include lack of integrity in government; the feeling that the individual no longer counts; the reality of material and spiritual poverty; the feeling that the grand American experiment is failing or has failed. I could recite these problems, and then I could sit down and offer no solutions. But I don't choose to do that either. The citizens of America expect more. They deserve and they want more than a recital of problems.

NOTES

Skill: Arguments and Claims

In paragraphs 2 and 3, Jordan claims that her presence is special and different. In paragraph 4, she uses her life and American history as evidence of this. She supports this evidence with reasoning. Jordan explains that the American Dream is a possibility for anyone to achieve. She is the first African American woman to give the keynote speech.

---

1. **party platform** a document or charter representing the party's official standpoints on major issues
2. **keynote speaker** the headlining speaker at a convention or meeting

Reading & Writing Companion

Skill:
Media

The text is serious here, but Jordan is speaking passionately. I can tell she really cares about America. She emphasizes "all of us" at the end, and she puts a pause between that and "are equal." She wanted to stress the idea that everyone is equal, not just some people.

Skill: Reasons and Evidence

Jordan quotes one of America's founding fathers. I know that "harmony" means "to work together," and "affection" means "love." Jordan uses Jefferson's words to support her claim that people should unify as a nation.

6   We are a people in a quandary about the present. We are a people in search of our future. We are a people in search of a national community. We are a people trying not only to solve the problems of the present, unemployment, inflation,[3] but we are attempting on a larger scale to fulfill the promise of America. We are attempting to fulfill our national purpose, to create and **sustain** a society in which all of us are equal.

. . .

7   And now we must look to the future. Let us heed the voice of the people and recognize their common sense. If we do not, we not only blaspheme our political heritage, we ignore the common ties that bind all Americans. Many fear the future. Many are distrustful of their leaders, and believe that their voices are never heard. Many seek only to satisfy their private wants; to satisfy their private interests. But this is the great danger America faces—that we will cease to be one nation and become instead a collection of interest groups: city against suburb, region against region, individual against individual; each seeking to satisfy private wants. If that happens, who then will speak for America? Who then will speak for the common good?

8   This is the question which must be answered in 1976: Are we to be one people bound together by common spirit, sharing in a common **endeavor;** or will we become a divided nation? For all of its uncertainty, we cannot flee the future. We must not become the "New Puritans" and reject our society. We must address and master the future together. It can be done if we restore the belief that we share a sense of national community, that we share a common national endeavor. It can be done.

9   There is no executive order;[4] there is no law that can require the American people to form a national community. This we must do as individuals, and if we do it as individuals, there is no President of the United States who can veto that decision.

10 As a first step, we must restore our belief in ourselves. We are a generous people, so why can't we be generous with each other? We need to take to heart the words spoken by Thomas Jefferson:

11 "Let us restore to social intercourse that harmony and that affection without which liberty and even life are but dreary things."

12 A nation is formed by the willingness of each of us to share in the responsibility for upholding the common good. A government is invigorated when each one of us is willing to participate in shaping the future of this nation. In this election year, we must define the "common good" and begin again to shape

---

3. **inflation** an increase in price and a decrease in the value of currency
4. **executive order** an act from the president that has the same impact as law but does not need congressional approval

a common future. Let each person do his or her part. If one citizen is unwilling to participate, all of us are going to suffer. For the American idea, though it is shared by all of us, is realized in each one of us.

13 And now, what are those of us who are elected public officials supposed to do? We call ourselves "public servants" but I'll tell you this: We as public servants must set an example for the rest of the nation. It is hypocritical for the public official to admonish and exhort the people to uphold the common good if we are derelict in upholding the common good. More is required of public officials than slogans and handshakes and press releases. More is required. We must hold ourselves strictly accountable. We must provide the people with a vision of the future.

14 If we promise as public officials, we must deliver. If we as public officials propose, we must produce. If we say to the American people, "It is time for you to be sacrificial"—sacrifice. If the public official says that, we [public officials] must be the first to give. We must be. And again, if we make mistakes, we must be willing to admit them. We have to do that. What we have to do is strike a balance between the idea that government should do everything and the idea, the belief, that government ought to do nothing. Strike a balance.

15 Let there be no **illusions** about the difficulty of forming this kind of a national community. It's tough, difficult, not easy. But a spirit of harmony will survive in America only if each of us remembers that we share a common destiny; if each of us remembers, when self-interest and bitterness seem to prevail, that we share a common destiny.

16 I have confidence that we can form this kind of national community.

• • •

17 I have that confidence.

18 We cannot improve on the system of government handed down to us by the founders of the Republic. There is no way to improve upon that. But what we can do is to find new ways to implement that system and realize our destiny.

19 Now I began this speech by commenting to you on the uniqueness of a Barbara Jordan making a keynote address. Well I am going to close my speech by quoting a Republican President and I ask you that as you listen to these words of Abraham Lincoln, relate them to the concept of a national community in which every last one of us participates:

20 "As I would not be a slave, so I would not be a master. This expresses my idea of Democracy. Whatever differs from this, to the extent of the difference, is no Democracy."

21 Thank you.

First Read

Read "All Together Now." After you read, complete the Think Questions below.

☁ THINK QUESTIONS

1. According to paragraph 4, Barbara Jordan's presence at the convention is evidence of what symbol?

2. List some of the problems that cause the American "people to feel cynical, angry, frustrated." Cite specific evidence from paragraph 5.

3. According to paragraph 13, who is supposed to set an example for the nation?

4. Find the word **deferred** in paragraph 4 of "All Together Now." Use context clues in the surrounding sentences, as well as the sentence in which the word appears, to determine the word's meaning. Write your definition here and identify clues that helped you figure out the meaning.

5. Use context clues to determine the meaning of **endeavor** as it is used in paragraph 8 of "All Together Now." Write your definition here and identify clues that helped you figure out the meaning. Then check the meaning in a dictionary.

Skill:
Arguments and Claims

Use the Checklist to analyze Arguments and Claims in "All Together Now." Refer to the sample student annotations about Arguments and Claims in the text.

••• CHECKLIST FOR ARGUMENTS AND CLAIMS

In order to trace the argument and specific claims, do the following:

- ✓ identify clues that reveal the author's opinion in the title, introduction, or conclusion

- ✓ note the first and last sentence of each body paragraph for specific claims that help to build the author's argument

- ✓ list the information the author introduces in sequential order

- ✓ use different colors to highlight and distinguish among an author's argument, claims, evidence, or reasons

- ✓ describe the author's argument in your own words

To evaluate the argument and specific claims, consider the following questions:

- ✓ Does the author support each claim with reasoning and evidence?

- ✓ Do the author's claims work together to support his or her overall argument?

- ✓ Which claims are not supported, if any?

Skill:
Arguments and Claims

Reread paragraphs 9–12 of "All Together Now." Then, using the Checklist on the previous page, answer the multiple-choice questions below.

↻ YOUR TURN

1. Barbara Jordan uses a quotation from Thomas Jefferson as evidence to support her claim that —

   ○ A. there is no law forcing Americans to form a national community.
   ○ B. the President of the United States can veto some decisions.
   ○ C. being kinder to others will help the country as a whole.
   ○ D. freedom is no longer inspiring to Americans.

2. This excerpt of the speech supports Jordan's overall argument by —

   ○ A. showing how much America has progressed in terms of civil rights.
   ○ B. showing the problems caused by divisive politics in America.
   ○ C. showing how willingness to work together will improve the government.
   ○ D. showing that politicians have gotten away with hypocrisy for far too long.

Skill:
Reasons and Evidence

Use the Checklist to analyze Reasons and Evidence in "All Together Now." Refer to the sample student annotations about Reasons and Evidence in the text.

••• CHECKLIST FOR REASONS AND EVIDENCE

In order to identify the reasons and evidence that support an author's claim(s) in an argument, note the following:

- ✓ the argument the author is making

- ✓ the claim or the main idea of the argument

- ✓ the reasons and evidence that support the claim and where they can be found

- ✓ if the evidence the author presents to support the claim is sound, or complete and comprehensive

- ✓ if there is sufficient evidence to support the claim or if more is needed

To assess whether the author's reasoning is sound and the evidence is relevant and sufficient, consider the following questions:

- ✓ What kind of argument is the author making?

- ✓ Is the reasoning, or the thinking behind the claims, sound and valid?

- ✓ Are the reasons and evidence the author presents to support the claim sufficient, or is more evidence needed? Why or why not?

Skill:
Reasons and Evidence

Reread paragraphs 18–21 of "All Together Now." Then, using the Checklist on the previous page, answer the multiple-choice questions below.

⟳ YOUR TURN

1. What type of evidence does Barbara Jordan use in this part of the speech?

   ○ A. the fact that the American system of government cannot be improved

   ○ B. statistics showing how unlikely it is for an African American woman to be asked to give a speech

   ○ C. an example of another national community that succeeds in making progress

   ○ D. a quotation from President Abraham Lincoln

2. Jordan emphasizes that Lincoln was a Republican because —

   ○ A. she is speaking to Democrats and wants to give an example of working with opponents.

   ○ B. she is speaking to Democrats and wants to mock Republicans.

   ○ C. she is speaking to Republicans and wants to insult Democrats.

   ○ D. she is speaking to Republicans and wants to inspire them.

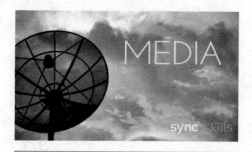

Skill:
Media

Use the Checklist to analyze Media in "All Together Now." Refer to the sample student annotations about Media in the text.

••• CHECKLIST FOR MEDIA

In order to determine how to compare and contrast a text to an audio, video, or multimedia version of the text, note the following:

- ✓ how the same topic can be treated, or presented, in more than one medium, such as audio, video, and multimedia versions of a text

- ✓ how treatments of a topic through different kinds of media can reveal more information about the topic

- ✓ which details are emphasized or absent in each medium, and the reasons behind these choices

- ✓ if similar details about the subject are emphasized, this may make the information seem more important or believable

- ✓ if different details are stressed, a reader or viewer may begin to think about the subject in a new way

To compare and contrast a text to an audio, video, or multimedia version of the text, analyzing each medium's portrayal of the subject, ask the following questions:

- ✓ How are the treatments of the source text similar? How are they different?

- ✓ How does each medium's portrayal affect the presentation of the subject?

- ✓ Why are different media able to emphasize or highlight certain kinds of information better than others?

Skill:
Media

Reread paragraphs 1–4 of "All Together Now" and then listen to the audio version of this portion of the speech. Complete the chart below by matching the correct sound element to the text excerpt and then explain how the sound element affects your understanding.

⟳ YOUR TURN

Sound Element	
A	Tone and Emphasis
B	Applause

Text Excerpt	Sound Element	Effect on Understanding
"It was one hundred and forty-four years ago that members of the Democratic Party first met in convention to select a Presidential candidate."	Dramatic Pause	The pauses after "ago" and "first" emphasize how long ago the first convention was. They also suggest that the convention is important and historic.
"I, Barbara Jordan, am a keynote speaker."		
"...one additional bit of evidence that the American Dream need not forever be deferred."		

Close Read

Reread "All Together Now." As you reread, complete the Skills Focus questions below. Then use your answers and annotations from the questions to help you complete the Write activity.

◎ SKILLS FOCUS

1. Identify a claim in the speech that supports Barbara Jordan's main argument. Explain her argument in your own words.

2. Identify and explain a type of evidence that Jordan uses to support her claim. Then give one example of additional evidence that she could add. Explain where in the structure of her argument she could incorporate this evidence.

3. Recall that Barbara Jordan raised her voice and paused when she said, "We are attempting to fulfill our national purpose, to create and sustain a society in which *all of us are equal*." Highlight this part of the speech and 1 or 2 other lines in which Jordan displays volume, tone, or another audio technique. Write a note explaining how Jordan's delivery impacted or changed your understanding of her argument or claim.

4. Find an example in the speech in which Barbara Jordan talks about the importance of national unity. Explain in your own words why the idea of national unity is worth pursuing.

✎ WRITE

DISCUSSION: Write notes to prepare for a collaborative conversation with a partner or a small group to discuss how to bring students in your community together in a positive way. First, establish a clear position by stating the most significant problem you see within the student community. Then provide reasons and evidence that support your arguments and claims. Finally, work together with your partner or group to reach a consensus about what actions students and staff should take to create a stronger student community.

Reading & Writing Companion   41

Mother Jones:
Fierce Fighter for Workers' Rights

INFORMATIONAL TEXT
Judith Pinkerton Josephson
1996

Introduction

Mary Harris Jones (1837–1930), known as Mother Jones, was an American schoolteacher and dressmaker who went on to become a prominent workers' rights activist and community organizer. This excerpt from author Judith Pinkerton Josephson's biography of the fearless crusader describes her groundbreaking demonstrations against unfair child labor practices and her historic 1903 march from Philadelphia to Sagamore Hill, New York, to protest the poor

"What about the little children from whom all song is gone?"

Copyright © BookheadEd Learning, LLC

from Chapter Nine: The March of the Mill Children[1]

1   "I love children," Mother Jones once told a reporter.

2   In countless shacks and shanties[2] across the country, she had tied the shoes of children, wiped their noses, hugged them while they cried, scrambled to find food for them, fought for their rights. By the turn of the century, almost two million children under the age of sixteen worked in mills, factories, and mines. Images of the child workers Mother Jones had seen stayed with her— the torn, bleeding fingers of the breaker boys,[3] the mill children living on coffee and stale bread.

3   In June 1903, Mother Jones went to Philadelphia, Pennsylvania—the heart of a **vast** textile industry. About one hundred thousand workers from six hundred different mills were on strike there. The strikers wanted their workweek cut from sixty to fifty-five hours, even if it meant lower wages. About a sixth of the strikers were children under sixteen.

4   Nationwide, eighty thousand children worked in the textile industry. In the South, Mother Jones had seen how dangerous their jobs were. Barefooted little girls and boys reached their tiny hands into the **treacherous** machinery to repair snapped threads or crawled underneath the machinery to oil it. At textile union headquarters, Mother Jones met more of these mill children. Their bodies were bone-thin, with hollow chests. Their shoulders were rounded from long hours spent hunched over the workbenches. Even worse, she saw "some with their hands off, some with the thumb missing, some with their fingers off at the knuckles"—victims of mill accidents.

5   Pennsylvania, like many other states, had laws that said children under thirteen could not work. But parents often lied about a child's age. Poor families either put their children to work in the mills or starved. Mill owners looked the other way, because child labor was cheap.

---

1. **Mill Children** children put to work in mills or factories
2. **shanties** small houses improvised from spare building materials and refuse
3. **breaker boys** workers, mostly children, employed to separate impurities from coal by hand after it is mined

NOTES

6 Mother Jones asked various newspaper publishers why they didn't write about child labor in Pennsylvania. The publishers told her they couldn't, since owners of the mills also owned stock in their newspapers. "Well, I've got stock in these little children," she said, "and I'll arrange a little publicity."

7 Mother Jones, now seventy-three, gathered a large group of mill children and their parents. She led them on a one-mile march from Philadelphia's Independence Square to its courthouse lawn. Mother Jones and a few children climbed up on a platform in front of a huge crowd. She held one boy's arm up high so the crowd could see his mutilated hand. "Philadelphia's mansions were built on the broken bones, the quivering hearts, and drooping heads of these children," she said. She lifted another child in her arms so the crowd could see how thin he was.

8 Mother Jones looked directly at the city officials standing at the open windows across the street. "Some day the workers will take possession of your city hall, and when we do, no child will be sacrificed on the altar of profit." Unmoved, the officials quickly closed their windows.

9 Local newspapers and some New York newspapers covered the event. How, Mother Jones wondered, could she draw national attention to the evils of child labor? Philadelphia's famous Liberty Bell, currently on a national tour and drawing huge crowds, gave her an idea. She and the textile union leaders would stage their own tour. They would march the mill children all the way to the president of the United States—Theodore Roosevelt. Mother Jones wanted the president to get Congress to pass a law that would take children out of the mills, mines, and factories, and put them in school.

10 When Mother Jones asked parents for permission to take their children with her, many hesitated. The march from Philadelphia to Sagamore Hill—the president's seaside mansion on Long Island near New York City—would cover 125 miles. It would be a difficult journey. But finally, the parents agreed. Many decided to come along on the march. Other striking men and women offered their help, too.

11 On July 7, 1903, nearly three hundred men, women, and children—followed by four wagons with supplies—began the long march. Newspapers carried daily reports of the march, calling the group "Mother Jones's Industrial Army," or "Mother Jones's Crusaders." The army was led by a fife-and-drum corps of three children dressed in Revolutionary War uniforms. Mother Jones wore her familiar, lace-fringed black dress. The marchers sang and carried flags, banners, and placards that read "We Want to Go to School!" "We Want Time to Play." **"Prosperity** is Here, Where is Ours?" "55 Hours or Nothing." "We Only Ask for Justice." "More Schools, Less Hospitals."

12 The temperature rose into the nineties. The roads were dusty, the children's shoes full of holes. Many of the young girls returned home. Some of the marchers walked only as far as the outskirts of Philadelphia. For the hundred or

so marchers who remained, this trip was an adventure in spite of the heat. They bathed and swam in brooks and rivers. Each of them carried a knapsack with a knife, fork, tin cup, and plate inside. Mother Jones took a huge pot for cooking meals on the way. Mother Jones also took along costumes, makeup, and jewelry so the children could stop in towns along the route and put on plays about the struggle of textile workers. The fife-and-drum corps gave concerts and passed the hat. People listened and donated money. Farmers met the marchers with wagonloads of fruit, vegetables, and clothes. Railroad engineers stopped their trains and gave them free rides. Hotel owners served free meals.

13 On July 10th, marchers camped across the Delaware River from Trenton, New Jersey. They had traveled about forty miles in three days. At first, police told the group they couldn't enter the city. Trenton mill owners didn't want any trouble. But Mother Jones invited the police to stay for lunch. The children gathered around the cooking pot with their tin plates and cups. The policemen smiled, talked kindly to them, and then allowed them to cross the bridge into Trenton. There Mother Jones spoke to a crowd of five thousand people. That night, the policemen's wives took the children into their homes, fed them, and packed them lunches for the next day's march.

14 By now, many of the children were growing weak. More returned home. Some adults on the march grumbled that Mother Jones just wanted people to notice *her*. They complained to reporters that Mother Jones often stayed in hotels while the marchers camped in hot, soggy tents filled with whining mosquitoes. Sometimes Mother Jones did stay in hotels, because she went ahead of the marchers to arrange for lodging and food in upcoming towns and to get publicity for the march.

15 As the remaining marchers pushed on to Princeton, New Jersey, a thunderstorm struck. Mother Jones and her army camped on the grounds of former President Grover Cleveland's estate. The Clevelands were away, and the caretaker let Mother Jones use the big, cool barn for a dormitory.

16 Mother Jones got permission from the mayor of Princeton to speak opposite the campus of Princeton University. Her topic: higher education. She spoke to a large crowd of professors, students, and residents. Pointing to one ten-year-old boy, James Ashworth, she said, "Here's a textbook on economics." The boy's body was stooped from carrying seventy-five-pound bundles of yarn. "He gets three dollars a week and his sister, who is fourteen, gets six dollars. They work in a carpet factory ten hours a day while the children of the rich are getting their higher education." Her piercing glance swept over the students in the crowd.

17 Mother Jones talked about children who could not read or write because they spent ten hours a day in Pennsylvania's silk mills. Those who hired these child workers used "the hands and feet of little children so they might buy automobiles for their wives and police dogs for their daughters to talk French to." She accused the mill owners of taking "babies almost from the cradle."

18   The next night, the marchers slept on the banks of the Delaware River. In every town, Mother Jones drew on what she did best—speaking—to gather support for her cause. One reporter wrote, "Mother Jones makes other speakers sound like tin cans."

19   Battling heat, rain, and swarms of mosquitoes at night, the marchers arrived in Elizabeth. Socialist party members helped house and feed the weary adults and children. The next morning, two businessmen gave Mother Jones her first car ride. She was delighted with this new "contraption."

20   On July 15, Mother Jones wrote a letter to President Roosevelt. She told him how these poor mill children lived, **appealed** to him as a father, and asked him to meet with her and the children. President Roosevelt did not answer Mother Jones's letter. Instead, he assigned secret service[4] officers to watch her. They thought she might be a threat to the president. That made her furious.

21   On July 24, after more than two weeks on the road, the marchers reached New York City. By now, just twenty marchers remained. One of them was Eddie Dunphy, a child whose job was to sit on a high stool eleven hours a day handing thread to another worker. For this he was paid three dollars a week. Mother Jones talked about Eddie and about Gussie Rangnew, a child who packed stockings in a factory. She too worked eleven hours a day for pennies.

22   At one meeting, a crowd of thirty thousand gathered. "We are quietly marching toward the president's home," she told the people. "I believe he can do something for these children, although the press **declares** he cannot."

23   One man wanted the children to have some fun while they were in New York City. Frank Bostick owned the wild animal show at Coney Island, an amusement park and resort. He invited the mill children to spend a day at the park. The children swam in the ocean and played along the beach.

24   When Frank Bostick's wild animal show ended that night, he let Mother Jones speak to the crowd that had attended. To add drama, she had some of the children crawl inside the empty cages. The smells of sawdust and animals hung in the air. But instead of lions and tigers, the cages held children. The children gripped the iron bars and solemnly stared out at the crowd while Mother Jones spoke.

25   "We want President Roosevelt to hear the wail of the children who never have a chance to go to school, but work eleven and twelve hours a day in the textile mills of Pennsylvania," she said, "who weave the carpets that he and you walk upon; and the lace curtains in your windows, and the clothes of the people."

26   She continued, "In Georgia where children work day and night in the cotton mills they have just passed a bill to protect songbirds. What about the little

---

4. **secret service** independent federal law enforcement

children from whom all song is gone?" After Mother Jones finished speaking, the crowd sat in stunned silence. In the distance, a lone lion roared.

27 The grueling walk had taken almost three weeks. Mother Jones had written the president twice with no answer. On July 29, she took three young boys to Sagamore Hill, where the president was staying. But the secret service stopped them at the mansion's gates. The president would not see them.

28 The group returned to New York City. Discouraged, Mother Jones reported her failure to the newspapers. Most of the marchers decided to return home. She stayed on briefly with the three children. Once more, she wrote President Roosevelt: "The child of today is the man or woman of tomorrow. . . . I have with me three children who have walked one hundred miles. . . . If you decide to see these children, I will bring them before you at any time you may set."

29 The president's secretary replied that the president felt that child labor was a problem for individual states to solve. "He is a brave guy when he wants to take a gun out and fight other grown people," said Mother Jones in disgust, "but when those children went to him, he could not see them."

30 In early August, Mother Jones finally took the last three children home. Soon after, the textile workers gave up and ended their strike. Adults and children went back to work, their working conditions unchanged.

31 Though she had not met with the president, Mother Jones had drawn the attention of the nation to the problem of child labor. She became even more of a national figure. Within a few years, Pennsylvania, New York, New Jersey, and other states did pass tougher child labor laws. The federal government finally passed a child labor law (part of the Fair Labor Standards Act) in 1938— thirty-five years after the march of the mill children.

©1997 by Judith Pinkerton Josephson, MOTHER JONES: FIERCE FIGHTER FOR WORKERS' RIGHTS. Reproduced by permission of Judith Pinkerton Josephson. Watch for the updated e-book of Mother Jones: Fierce Fighter for Workers' Rights as part of the Spotlight Biography Series (eFrog Press) in Spring 2015. Also see www.JudithJosephson.com.

✏ WRITE

PERSONAL RESPONSE: Do you think Mother Jones was an effective leader? Write a brief response to this question. Remember to cite evidence from the text to support your response.

Speech to the Young: Speech to the Progress-Toward

POETRY
Gwendolyn Brooks
1932

Introduction

Highly regarded and widely admired, Gwendolyn Brooks (1917–2000) was the poet laureate of Illinois and the first African American to win the Pulitzer Prize. In her poem "Speech to the Young: Speech to the Progress-Toward," the speaker gives wise advice to young people about how to live life.

"even if you are not ready for day it cannot always be night."

NOTES

1   Say to them,
2   say to the down-**keepers**,
3   the sun-**slappers**,
4   the self-**soilers**,
5   the **harmony-hushers**,
6   "even if you are not ready for day
7   it cannot always be night."
8   You will be right.
9   For that is the hard home-run.
10   Live not for battles won.
11   Live not for the-end-of-the-song.
12   Live in the along.

"Speech to the Young: Speech to the Progress-Toward" by Gwendolyn Brooks. Reprinted by Consent of Brooks Permissions.

✏ WRITE

POETRY: Write a poem in response to "Speech to the Young: Speech to the Progress-Toward" about how it feels to achieve the "hard home-run" that Brooks mentions. Use poetic elements and structure as you craft your poem.

Please note that excerpts and passages in the StudySync® library and this workbook are intended as touchstones to generate interest in an author's work. The excerpts and passages do not substitute for the reading of entire texts, and StudySync® strongly recommends that students seek out and purchase the whole literary or informational work in order to experience it as the author intended. Links to online resellers are available in our digital library. In addition, complete works may be ordered through an authorized reseller by filling out and returning to StudySync® the order form enclosed in this workbook.

Reading & Writing Companion   49

Letter to President Theodore Roosevelt, July 17, 1903

ARGUMENTATIVE TEXT
Mother Jones
1903

Introduction

In June of 1903, a textile strike in Philadelphia saw 90,000 workers walk off the job in order to fight for better conditions. Sixteen thousand of these workers were children under the age of 16. News coverage of the strike was scarce, due in large part to the common business interests shared by textile mill owners and news publishers. On July 7, labor leader "Mother" Mary Harris Jones, otherwise known as Mother Jones (1837–1930), announced her plan to march with dozens of children from Philadelphia to Roosevelt's home outside New York City, hoping to draw attention to the harsh conditions experienced by children working in factories. One week into their march, on July 17, 1903, Jones wrote this public letter to President Roosevelt. After receiving no response, Mother Jones wrote to the president once again. She finally received a letter from Roosevelt's secretary, stating that the issue was under the jurisdiction of the states, and that the president would not meet with Mother Jones and her fellow marchers.

"... no child shall die of hunger at the will of any manufacturer in this fair land."

To Theodore Roosevelt
President of the United States
Dear Sir:

1   Being citizens of the United States of America, we, members of the textile industry, take the liberty of addressing this **appeal** to you. As Chief Executive of the United States, you are, in a sense, our father and leader, and as such we look to you for advice and guidance. Perhaps the crime of child slavery has never been forcibly brought to your notice.

Mary Harris "Mother" Jones led a multi-week strike to advocate the end of child labor and harsh factory conditions. Here, child workers pose for a photograph during a strike in Philadelphia, PA, circa 1890.

2   Yet, as father of us all, surely the smallest detail must be of interest to you. In Philadelphia, Pa., there are ninety thousand (90,000) textile workers who are on **strike**, asking for a reduction from sixty to fifty-five hours a week. With machinery, Mr. President, we believe that forty-eight hours is sufficient.

3   If the United States Senate had passed the eight-hour bill,[1] this strike might not have occurred. We also ask that the children be taken from the industrial prisons of this nation, and given their right of attending schools, so that in years to come better citizens will be given to this republic.

4   These little children, raked by cruel toil beneath the iron wheels of greed, are starving in this country which you have declared is in the height of **prosperity**— slaughtered, ten hours a day, every day in the week, every week in the month, every month in the year, that our manufacturing aristocracy[2] may live to **exploit** more slaves as the years roll by.

---

1. **eight-hour bill** the ideal of an eight-hour workday ultimately enshrined in law by the Fair Labor Standards Act of 1938, which established the forty-hour week and overtime for all industries engaged in interstate commerce
2. **manufacturing aristocracy** wealthy factory owners

NOTES

Skill: Language, Style, and Audience

In the first paragraph, the writer refers to Roosevelt as the "father and leader" of our country and asks for his guidance and advice around the "crime of child slavery." This creates an emotional response for the audience. Although the letter is addressed to President Roosevelt, it was written for the public.

Copyright © BookheadEd Learning, LLC

Skill: Author's Purpose and Point of View

In paragraph 4, Mother Jones brings up the factory owners, saying they "live to exploit" children. These are harsh words and show that her position is the morally correct one.

She also uses a lot of emotional words and addresses Roosevelt directly with the word "you." She is trying to persuade the president and others to protect the children in factories.

5   We ask you, Mr. President, if our commercial[3] greatness has not cost us too much by being built upon the quivering hearts of helpless children? We who know of these sufferings have taken up their cause and are now marching toward you in the hope that your tender heart will counsel with us to abolish this crime.

6   The manufacturers have threatened to starve these children, and we seek to show that no child shall die of hunger at the will of any manufacturer in this fair land. The clergy, whose work this really is, are silent on the crime of ages, and so we appeal to you.

7   It is in the hope that the words of Christ will be more clearly interpreted by you when he said "Suffer little children to come unto me." Our destination is New York City, and after that Oyster Bay.[4] As your children, may we hope to have the pleasure of an audience? We only ask that you advise us as to the best course.

8   In Philadelphia alone thousands of persons will wait upon your answer, while throughout the land, wherever there is organized labor, the people will anxiously await an expression of your **sentiments** toward suffering childhood.

9   On behalf of these people, we beg that you will reply and let us know whether we may expect an audience.

10   The reply should be addressed to "Mother" Jones's Crusaders, en route according to the daily papers.

11   We are very respectfully yours,

"Mother" Jones, Chairman

---

3. **commercial** related to commerce, trade, and general business activities intended to make profit
4. **Oyster Bay** a municipality of Long Island, New York

First Read

Read "Letter to President Theodore Roosevelt, July 17, 1903." After you read, complete the Think Questions below.

☁ THINK QUESTIONS

1. What does Mother Jones hope to accomplish with this letter? Explain any specific goals she mentions in the text.

2. What does Mother Jones mean by "industrial prisons" in paragraph 3 of the text? Cite any other places in the letter that help you to make an inference about the meaning of this term. Use evidence to support your understanding of this term's meaning.

3. Why does Mother Jones reach out directly to President Roosevelt? Describe why her previous efforts to stand up for child laborers were unsuccessful.

4. Read the following dictionary entry:

strike

strike \ strīk\

noun

a. a sudden military attack

b. a collective refusal to work organized by a group of employees

verb

c. to hit someone purposefully and forcefully

d. (of a disaster, disease or other problem) to occur suddenly and cause harm

Which definition most closely matches the meaning of **strike** as it is used in paragraph 2? Write the correct definition of *strike* here and explain how you figured out the proper meaning.

5. Based on context clues, what is the meaning of the word **exploit** as it is used in paragraph 4? Write your best definition of *exploit* here, explaining how you figured it out.

Please note that excerpts and passages in the StudySync® library and this workbook are intended as touchstones to generate interest in an author's work. The excerpts and passages do not substitute for the reading of entire texts, and StudySync® strongly recommends that students seek out and purchase the whole literary or informational work in order to experience it as the author intended. Links to online resellers are available in our digital library. In addition, complete works may be ordered through an authorized reseller by filling out and returning to StudySync® the order form enclosed in this workbook.

Reading & Writing Companion   **53**

Skill: Language, Style, and Audience

Use the Checklist to analyze Language, Style, and Audience in "Letter to President Theodore Roosevelt, July 17, 1903." Refer to the sample student annotations about Language, Style, and Audience in the text.

••• CHECKLIST FOR LANGUAGE, STYLE, AND AUDIENCE

In order to determine an author's style, do the following:

- ✓ identify and define any unfamiliar words or phrases

- ✓ use context, including the meaning of surrounding words and phrases

- ✓ note possible reactions to the author's word choice

- ✓ examine your reaction to the author's word choice and how the author's word choice affected your reaction

To analyze the impact of specific word choice on meaning and tone, ask the following questions:

- ✓ How did your understanding of the language change during your analysis?

- ✓ What stylistic choices can you identify in the text? How does the style influence your understanding of the language?

- ✓ How could various audiences interpret this language? What different possible emotional responses can you list?

- ✓ How does the writer's choice of words impact or create a specific tone in the text?

Skill: Language, Style, and Audience

Reread paragraphs 2–3 of "Letter to President Theodore Roosevelt, July 17, 1903." Then, using the Checklist on the previous page, answer the multiple-choice questions below.

⟳ YOUR TURN

1. This question has two parts. First, answer Part A. Then, answer Part B.

    Part A: By choosing to use strong, descriptive language in her letter, Mother Jones is—

    ○ A. mocking President Roosevelt for his ineffective leadership.
    ○ B. encouraging readers to write letters to their senators for help.
    ○ C. attempting to make a heartfelt appeal to President Roosevelt.
    ○ D. saying the government and Roosevelt cannot be relied on to reform the textile industry.

    Part B: What evidence from the text BEST supports your response to Part A?

    ○ A. In Philadelphia, Pa., there are ninety thousand (90,000) textile workers who are on strike.
    ○ B. Yet, as father of us all, surely the smallest detail must be of interest to you.
    ○ C. If the United States Senate had passed the eight-hour bill, this strike might not have occurred.
    ○ D. asking for a reduction from sixty to fifty-five hours a week

Skill: Author's Purpose and Point of View

Use the Checklist to analyze Author's Purpose and Point of View in "Letter to President Theodore Roosevelt, July 17, 1903." Refer to the sample student annotations about Author's Purpose and Point of View in the text.

••• CHECKLIST FOR AUTHOR'S PURPOSE AND POINT OF VIEW

In order to identify author's purpose and point of view, note the following:

✓ facts, statistics, and graphic aids, as these indicate that the author is writing to inform

✓ descriptive or sensory details and emotional language may indicate that the author is writing to describe and dramatize events

✓ descriptions that present a complicated process in plain language may indicate that the author is writing to explain

✓ emotional language with a call to action may indicate that the author is trying to persuade readers or stress an opinion

✓ the language the author uses can also hold clues to the author's point of view on a subject or topic

To determine the author's purpose and point of view in a text, consider the following questions:

✓ How does the author convey, or communicate, information in the text?

✓ Does the author use figurative or emotional language? How does it affect the purpose and point of view?

✓ How does the author distinguish his or her perspective or point of view?

✓ Does the author bring up different points of view? How is the author's position or point of view different from opposing points of view?

Skill: Author's Purpose and Point of View

Reread paragraphs 6–9 of "Letter to President Theodore Roosevelt, July 17, 1903." Then, using the Checklist on the previous page, answer the multiple-choice questions below.

↻ YOUR TURN

1. Which piece of evidence helps to distinguish Mother Jones's position as the position of working people, children, and their families?

   ○ A. "The manufacturers have threatened to starve these children . . ."
   ○ B. "The clergy, whose work this really is, are silent on the crime of ages . . ."
   ○ C. "It is in the hope that the words of Christ will be more clearly interpreted by you . . ."
   ○ D. "On behalf of these people, we beg you will reply . . ."

2. What do words like *suffer* and *hope* suggest about a reason why Mother Jones wrote her letter?

   ○ A. to inform readers about the unfair working condition with facts
   ○ B. to encourage readers to write letters to their senators for help
   ○ C. to persuade readers and stress her opinion by using emotional words
   ○ D. to explain the processes in the textile industry with descriptions

Close Read

Reread "Letter to President Theodore Roosevelt, July 17, 1903." As you reread, complete the Skills Focus questions below. Then use your answers and annotations from the questions to help you complete the Write activity.

⊚ SKILLS FOCUS

1. Recall that a claim is a main idea in an argumentative text. Identify one claim the author makes, and rewrite the claim in your own words.

2. Identify evidence that shows the author's purpose in writing this text. Explain what audience the author is writing to and what reasons she has for writing.

3. In the poem "Speech to the Young: Speech to the Progress-Toward," the speaker uses the pronoun *you* in these lines: "even if you are not ready for day / it cannot always be night." In the letter, Mother Jones also uses the pronoun *you* to directly address the intended audience. Identify an example of the pronoun *you* in the letter. Compare and contrast how the pronoun *you* is used in the

letter and the poem. In your response, explain who is being addressed by the pronoun *you* and the message each writer is trying to express.

4. Identify examples of emotional language that Mother Jones used to try to persuade the president to support her cause. How does this language help distinguish Mother Jones's position from others, including the factory owners?

5. Identify evidence that shows Mother Jones's dream for the future. Explain whether you think her dream was worth pursuing.

✏ WRITE

COMPARE AND CONTRAST: Compare and contrast the intended audience and the purpose in the excerpt from *Mother Jones: Fierce Fighter for Workers' Rights*, "Speech to the Young: Speech to the Progress-Toward," and "Letter to President Theodore Roosevelt, July 17, 1903." Why did the authors write these texts? Explain how the audience and the purpose of each text impact its style and language.

Before We Were Free

FICTION
Julia Alvarez
2002

Introduction

Essayist, poet, and novelist Julia Alvarez (b. 1950) has earned commercial and critical success, most notably with the novels *How the Garcia Girls Lost Their Accents*, *In the Time of the Butterflies* and *Yo!* Much of Alvarez's work is inspired by her sudden move from the Dominican Republic to New York in 1960, after her father's role in a failed plot against the dictator Rafael Trujillo led Alvarez's family to flee. *Before We Were Free* takes a page from the author's own childhood, as narrator Anita de la Torre and her older siblings, Lucinda and Mundín, try to get to the bottom of why the military police (SIM) are watching their family's house. The novel is interested in, as Alvarez explains it, "the sons and daughters of those who had been tortured, imprisoned, or murdered—kids like my cousins and my

"We just have to act as if the SIM aren't there and carry on with normal life."

NOTES

from Chapter 2

1   Lucinda and I wait in her room, listening at the door, tense with **concentration**. When we don't hear noises anymore, Lucinda turns the knob carefully, and we tiptoe out into the hall.

2   The SIM seem to have left. We spot Chucha crossing the patio toward the front of the house, a broom over her shoulder like a rifle. She looks like she's going to shoot the SIM for tracking mud on her clean floors.

3   "Chucha!" We wave to her to come talk to us.

4   "Where's Mami?" I ask, feeling the same mounting panic I felt earlier when Mami left with the SIM. "Is she okay?"

5   "She's on the *teléfono*, calling Don Mundo," Chucha explains.

6   "What about . . . ?" Lucinda wrinkles her nose instead of saying their names.

7   "*Esos animales*," Chucha says, shaking her head. Those animals, the SIM, searched every house in the **compound**, getting more and more destructive when they didn't find what they were looking for, tromping through Chucha's room, turning over her coffin and tearing off the velvet lining. They also stormed through Porfirio's and Ursulina's rooms. "Those two are so terrified," Chucha concludes, "they are packing their things and leaving the house."

8   But the SIM stay. They sit in their black Volkswagens at the top of our drive, blocking our way out.

9   At dinner, Papi says everything will be fine. We just have to act as if the SIM aren't there and carry on with normal life. But I notice that, like the rest of us, he doesn't eat a single bite. And is it really normal that Mami and Papi have us all sleep on mattresses on their bedroom floor with the door locked?

Skill:
Setting

The story is set in a compound of houses. The SIM have invaded "every house in the compound" by "tromping" and storming through rooms. This must be why Chucha is angry at the secret police.

10 We lie in the dark, talking in whispers, Mundín on a mat by himself, Lucinda and I on a larger mattress, and Papi and Mami on theirs they placed right beside ours.

11 "How come you don't just stay up on your bed?" I ask.

12 "Keep your voice down," Mami reminds me.

13 "Okay, okay," I whisper. But I still don't get an answer. "And what about Chucha?" I ask. "She's all by herself at the back of the house."

14 "Don't worry," Mundín says, "I don't think a bullet can get through that coffin!"

15 "Bullets!" I sit right up in bed.

16 "Shhhh!" my whole family reminds me.

17 Those black cars sit there for days and days—sometimes there's only one, sometimes as many as three. Every morning, when Papi leaves for the office, one of the cars starts up its colicky motor and follows him down the hill. In the evening, when he comes home, it comes back with him. I don't know when those SIM ever go to their own houses to eat their suppers and talk with their kids.

18 "Are they really policemen?" I keep asking Mami. It doesn't make any sense. If the SIM are policemen, secret or not, shouldn't we trust them instead of being afraid of them? But all Mami will say is "Shhh!" Meanwhile, we can't go to school because something might happen to us. "Like what?" I ask. Like what Chucha said about people disappearing? Is that what Mami worries will happen to us? "Didn't Papi say we should carry on with normal life?"

19 "Anita, *por favor*," Mami pleads, collapsing in a hall chair. She leans forward and whispers in my ear, "Please, please, you must stop asking questions."

20 "But why?" I whisper back. I can smell her shampoo, which smells like coconuts in her hair.

21 "Because I don't have any answers," she replies.

22 Not that Mami is the only one I try talking to.

23 My brother, Mundín, who's two years older, sometimes explains things to me. But this time when I ask him what's going on, he looks worried and whispers, "Ask Papi." He's biting his nails again, something he stopped doing when he turned fourteen in August.

24 I try asking Papi.

Please note that excerpts and passages in the StudySync® library and this workbook are intended as touchstones to generate interest in an author's work. The excerpts and passages do not substitute for the reading of entire texts, and StudySync® strongly recommends that students seek out and purchase the whole literary or informational work in order to experience it as the author intended. Links to online resellers are available in our digital library. In addition, complete works may be ordered through an authorized reseller by filling out and returning to StudySync® the order form enclosed in this workbook.

Reading & Writing Companion

61

Skill:
Setting

The narrator follows her father to the living room, where he talks to people on the phone. But even here in the living room, he speaks in code. This creates a feeling of danger and suspense. I can see this in the father's reaction.

25 One evening when the phone rings, I follow him into our living room. I hear him say something about some butterflies in a car accident.

26 "Butterflies in a car accident?" I ask, puzzled.

27 He seems startled that I'm in the room. "What are you doing here?" he snaps. I put my hands on my hips. "Honestly, Papi! I live here!" I can't believe he's asking me what I'm doing in our own living room! Of course, he immediately apologizes. "Sorry, *amorcito*, you startled me." His eyes are moist, as if he's holding back tears.

28 "So what about those butterflies, Papi?"

29 "They're not real butterflies," he explains softly. "It's just . . . a nickname for some very special ladies who had an . . . accident last night."

30 "What kind of an accident? And why are they called butterflies anyhow? Don't they have a real name?"

31 Again a shhh.

32 My last **resort** is asking Lucinda. My older sister has been in a vile mood since the SIM cornered us in our own house. Lucinda loves parties and talking on the phone, and she hates being cooped up. She spends most of the time in her room, trying out so many hairstyles that I'm sure that when we finally leave the compound and go to the United States of America, Lucinda will be bald.

33 "Lucinda, por favor, pretty please, tell me what is going on?" I promise her a back rub that she doesn't have to pay me for.

34 Lucinda puts her hairbrush down on her vanity and makes a sign for me to follow her to the patio out back.

35 "We should be okay out here," she whispers, looking over her shoulder.

36 "Why are you whispering?" In fact, everyone has been talking in whispers and low voices this last week, as if the house is full of fussy babies who've finally fallen asleep.

37 Lucinda explains. The SIM have probably hidden microphones in the house and are monitoring our conversations from their VWs.[1]

38 "Why are they treating us like criminals? We haven't done anything wrong."

---

1. **VWs** Volkswagens

39 "Shhh!" Lucinda hushes me. For a moment she looks doubtful about continuing to explain things to a little sister who can't keep her voice down. "It's all about T-O-N-I," she says, spelling out our uncle's name in English. "A few months ago, he and his friends were involved in a **plot** to get rid of our dictator."

40 "You mean. . . ." I don't even have to say our leader's name. Lucinda nods solemnly and puts a finger to her lips.

41 Now I'm really confused. I thought we liked El Jefe.[2] His picture hangs in our front entryway with the saying below it: IN THIS HOUSE, TRUJILLO RULES. "But if he's so bad, why does Mrs. Brown hang his picture in our classroom next to George Washington?"

42 "We have to do that. Everyone has to. He's a dictator."

43 I'm not really sure what a dictator does. But this is probably not a good time to ask.

44 It turns out that the SIM discovered the plot and most of our uncle's friends were arrested. As for Tío Toni, nobody knows where he is. "He might be hiding out or they"—Lucinda looks over her shoulder. I know just who she means—"they might have him in custody."

45 "Will they disappear him?"

46 Lucinda seems surprised that I know about such matters. "Let's hope not," she sighs. Tío Toni is a special favorite of hers. At twenty-four, he's not that much older than she, at fifteen, and he is very handsome. All her girlfriends have crushes on him. "Ever since the SIM uncovered that plot, they've been after the family. That's why everyone's left. Tío Carlos and Mamita and Papito —"

47 "Why don't we leave, too, since we're not going to school anyway?"

48 "And **abandon** Tío Toni?" Lucinda shakes her head vigorously. Her pretty auburn hair is up in this hairdo called a chignon, like Princess Grace wears in her magazine wedding pictures. It comes undone and cascades down her back. "What if he comes back? What if he needs our help?" Her voice has risen above her usual whispering.

49 For once in the last few weeks, it's my turn to tell someone else in our house, "SHHHH!"

Excerpted from Before We Were Free by Julia Alvarez, published by Laurel-Leaf Books.

---

2. **El Jefe** (Spanish) the chief or boss

First Read

Read *Before We Were Free*. After you read, complete the Think Questions below.

 THINK QUESTIONS

1. Why are Lucinda and the narrator listening tensely for noises at the beginning of the excerpt? Explain.

2. How does the narrator's family often respond when the narrator asks questions? Give examples.

3. Why do the narrator and Lucinda whisper about "T-O-N-I"? Explain, citing specific evidence.

4. Read the following dictionary entry:

compound

com•pound \'käm'pound\

noun

a. a thing that is composed of at least two separate elements
b. a group of buildings or residences in one fenced-in area

verb

c. to put together or form by combining parts
d. to make a problem worse or more intensified

Which definition most closely matches the meaning of **compound** as it is used in paragraph 7? Write the correct definition of *compound* here, and explain how you figured out the correct meaning.

5. Based on context clues, what is the meaning of the word **resort** as it is used in paragraph 32? Write your best definition of *resort* here, explaining how you figured it out.

 **SETTING**

sync skills

Skill:
Setting

Use the Checklist to analyze Setting in *Before We Were Free*. Refer to the sample student annotations about Setting in the text.

••• CHECKLIST FOR SETTING

In order to identify how particular elements of a story interact, note the following:

- ✓ the setting of the story

- ✓ the characters in the text and the problems they face

- ✓ how the events of the plot unfold, and how that affects the setting and characters

- ✓ how the setting shapes the characters and plot

- ✓ cite the specific words, phrases, sentences, paragraphs, or images from the text that support your analysis

To analyze how particular elements of a story interact, consider the following questions as a guide:

- ✓ What is the setting(s) of the story?

- ✓ How does the setting affect the characters and plot?

- ✓ How does the setting contribute to or help solve the conflict?

- ✓ How do the characters' decisions affect the plot and setting(s)?

Please note that excerpts and passages in the StudySync® library and this workbook are intended as touchstones to generate interest in an author's work. The excerpts and passages do not substitute for the reading of entire texts, and StudySync® strongly recommends that students seek out and purchase the whole literary or informational work in order to experience it as the author intended. Links to online resellers are available in our digital library. In addition, complete works may be ordered through an authorized reseller by filling out and returning to StudySync® the order form enclosed in this workbook.

Reading & Writing
Companion   65

Skill:
Setting

Reread paragraphs 32–39 from *Before We Were Free*. Then, using the Checklist on the previous page, answer the multiple-choice questions below.

⟳ YOUR TURN

1. In this section of the story, the setting changes from —

   ○ A. Lucinda's bedroom to the patio.
   ○ B. a party to Lucinda's bedroom.
   ○ C. the compound to the patio.
   ○ D. the patio to a car.

2. Based on textual evidence, the reader can conclude that Lucinda wants to talk somewhere else because she —

   ○ A. hates being cooped up inside the house.
   ○ B. thinks the SIM will not be able to hear what they say on the patio.
   ○ C. finds it to be cooler outside on the patio.
   ○ D. worries that her parents will be upset if they hear what she says.

3. In paragraph 36, why does the narrator say that it seems "as if the house is full of fussy babies who've finally fallen asleep"?

   ○ A. People in the house are talking in a low voice because they are afraid of being heard by someone else.
   ○ B. People in the house are acting childish because they are tense.
   ○ C. The family members have been having trouble sleeping.
   ○ D. The family is taking care of the children of people who have left.

Close Read

Reread *Before We Were Free*. As you reread, complete the Skills Focus questions below. Then use your answers and annotations from the questions to help you complete the Write activity.

◎ SKILLS FOCUS

1. Identify a detail that shows a change in the setting of the story. Then explain how this change of setting affects character and plot development.

2. Reread paragraph 7. Identify a detail about how some people in the compound are reacting to the secret police (SIM). Explain how this example helps you understand a conflict in the story.

3. Identify an example of language the author uses to create suspense. Explain how this example advances the plot.

4. Reread the dialogue in paragraphs 12–16. How do the characters' words and actions contribute to the mood or feeling of the story? Explain how this mood or feeling is related to the conflict.

5. Identify a detail that supports the idea that staying in the compound is worth it despite the inconveniences and dangers. Explain whether you agree or disagree that the ideal of staying loyal to family members is worth taking risks.

✏ WRITE

LITERARY ANALYSIS: Although Papi says, "Everything will be fine" regarding the secret police (SIM), Alvarez describes a feeling of omnipresent terror in the de la Torre household. Identify and analyze how the setting shows that Papi and the others are afraid and/or have something to fear. Be sure to use textual evidence to support your response.

Please note that excerpts and passages in the StudySync® library and this workbook are intended as touchstones to generate interest in an author's work. The excerpts and passages do not substitute for the reading of entire texts, and StudySync® strongly recommends that students seek out and purchase the whole literary or informational work in order to experience it as the author intended. Links to online resellers are available in our digital library. In addition, complete works may be ordered through an authorized reseller by filling out and returning to StudySync® the order form enclosed in this workbook.

Reading & Writing Companion   **67**

Machines, not people, should be exploring the stars for now

ARGUMENTATIVE TEXT
Don Lincoln
2017

Introduction

Don Lincoln, Ph.D. (b. 1964) is an American physicist who is best known for research that led to important discoveries within the field of physics. In this text, Lincoln adds to the conversation about robotic versus manned space travel and presents arguments meant to help people consider where the space program ought to direct its attention in the future.

[handwritten top margin: persuasive, robots firsts]

"We have dreamed of a time when humans can travel through space . . . "

NOTES

1 In the last several weeks, two events demanded the attention of space enthusiasts. On March 30, entrepreneur Elon Musk's Space X company successfully reused a previously flown rocket to launch a communication satellite into space. And on April 6, American space **pioneer** John Glenn was laid to rest.

2 In their own way, Musk and Glenn each represent the hopes and dreams of those who delight in the idea of mankind leaving the bounds of Earth and exploring the solar system and, ultimately, the stars.

3 Over the past 50 years, we've seen men first orbit the globe and then walk on the moon. We were gripped by the fictional journeys of the Starship Enterprise, which explored the galaxy, encountering new life and new civilizations. Popcorn in hand, we watched Matt Damon struggle to survive in "The Martian."

> Skill: Greek and
> Latin Affixes and
> Roots

4 We have dreamed of a time when humans can travel through space as readily as when early mariners[1] unfurled their sails and headed west in search of new lands. But we might not have stopped and asked an important question.

5 Should we be doing that? *[handwritten: should we send people to other planet]*

6 Now, I am not asking whether we should explore the universe. I also dream of the day that we become galactic citizens. The question is whether the initial exploration of space should be done by humans or by robots. I would argue that, for the moment, robotic exploration should have the upper hand.

[handwritten: Robots should go to space first]

7 Proponents of the astronaut-preferred camp point, quite rightfully, at the versatility and independence of humans. Fans of human spaceflight are certainly correct when they remind us that humans are highly versatile. People observe the conditions around them and can react to circumstances as needed.

8 However, people are also fragile. They need food, water, and air. They can exist in only a narrow range of temperatures and find **inhospitable** both

[handwritten: Reason]

Galactic looks like galaxy, so the words could have the same root and a similar meaning. I know the suffix -ic forms adjectives. Based on these clues, I think the word galactic might describe things in space. I'll check the dictionary to be sure.

---

1. **mariners** people who work as sailors

Skill: Reasons
and Evidence

Lincoln claims that manned missions are expensive. He uses many examples and numerical evidence from past trips to prove this. He then warns how expensive a manned trip to Mars would be.

Lincoln's reasoning is strong and valid. Spending too much money is usually a bad thing. Plus, he points out that a manned mission could hurt the rest of the space program. Overall, his reasoning supports the idea that robots, not humans, should be exploring space.

vacuums and a radioactive environment. While some adventurers might prefer to remain in space forever, many of them expect to land gently back on Earth. All of these considerations are extremely challenging and not important for robotic missions. *] Reason | humans need form of things to survive*

9 Engineering spacecraft that satisfies human requirements is also very expensive. The International Space Station cost about $170 billion (all costs given in 2017 dollars), resulting only in a large facility locked in a low earth orbit. The storied Apollo missions included a **mere** six lunar landings, at an inflation-adjusted cost of $120 billion.

10 Possible manned missions to Mars are imagined to cost about $1 trillion, with the outcome being limited exploration of the Red Planet by about 2030 (with some estimates saying 2050). And a mission with that price tag would hamstring[2] the rest of the space program.

11 In contrast, robotic exploration of the solar system is far less costly. The Cassini mission to Saturn cost about $3.2 billion. The Mars Curiosity Rover cost about $2.5 billion. These and other missions have been wildly successful in teaching us about places where literally no one has gone before. Mars missions have explored ancient streams where knee-deep water once flowed and have found organic carbon[3] embedded in surface rocks.

12 In addition, there are methods for exploring the cosmos that don't require actually going to the place under study. The Hubble telescope has perhaps revealed more about the universe than any other scientific instrument, cost about $14 billion, including imaging the first galaxies formed, and played a key role in the discovery that the expansion of the universe is **accelerating**. And the wildly successful planet-hunting Kepler satellite weighs in at under $1 billion.

Reason 2 Money

13 Manned programs can cost tens or hundreds of times more than the robotic missions.

14 But it's not just about the money. There are three important goals we need to achieve from our space program. The first is monitoring our own world, resulting in storm warnings and help in understanding our complex planet, which can best be done by tireless satellites orbiting the Earth. The second is to learn more about our solar system and the more distant universe. On this, the case is also clear: robotic exploration, through either space probes or telescopes, provides a much better yield for much lower money.

2. **hamstring** (verb) to foil or prevent an effort from succeeding
3. **organic carbon** carbon found in soil or other natural matter

15 The final goal is that of making humanity a multiplanetary species. By definition, this includes manned spaceflight, but the question is really how we should achieve that objective.

16 (Developing human space-faring technology is **crucial**, but first we need to decide where to go. The moon is a dead planet and Mars is not nearly as welcoming as the New World was to the Spanish explorers. In fact, there is no place in our solar system where pioneers can simply drop seeds in the soil and wait for food to pop out of the ground. For that, we need to look at distant stars.

Skill: Technical Language

Interstellar sounds like a term that is related to space. The previous sentence was about stars, and *inter-* means "between or among," so I think this part means "exploring among the stars." The term makes me think that this is an informative essay, meant to be authoritative.

17 And interstellar exploration is also something in which robots will lead the way. Following the identification of a possibly habitable planet by the Kepler satellite or perhaps PLATO, a European Space Agency planet-hunting telescope scheduled to be launched in 2024, the next step would be a survey of the planetary system by an unmanned probe.)

Reason 3   robots should go first to find place where econ live

18 This might be patterned after billionaire investor Yuri Milner's Breakthrough Starshot, or some other approach. Here, expected advances in artificial intelligence will become crucial. A round-trip radio signal to Proxima Centauri, our nearest stellar neighbor, will take eight years. *) Reason 3*

19 And if we chose to explore the nearest sun-like star, the signal transit time is more like 24 years. With a multiyear time lag between messages, the interstellar probe will have to be able to execute independent judgment.

20 Only once a habitable planet is identified by these robotic approaches, will it be the time for a manned mission. With a welcoming destination beckoning to them, a team of intrepid men and women will leave the solar system and strike out for a new home. And, at that moment, *homo interstellaris*[4] will come of age. *) Reason 4   time*

4. **homo interstellaris** the projected human beings of future space exploration

First Read

Read "Machines, not people, should be exploring the stars for now." After you read, complete the Think Questions below.

☁ THINK QUESTIONS

1. Why does the author believe that robotic space exploration is better than manned space exploration for now? Provide two pieces of evidence from the text to support your answer.

2. What do humans need to travel in space that robots do not need? Provide examples from the text to support your answer.

3. According to the author, what are the three most important goals of the space program?

4. Use context clues to determine the meaning of **inhospitable** as it is used in paragraph 8 of "Machines, not people, should be exploring the stars for now." Write your definition here and identify clues that helped you figure out the meaning. Then check the meaning in a dictionary.

5. Find the word **mere** in paragraph 9 of "Machines, not people, should be exploring the stars for now." Use context clues in the surrounding sentences, as well as the sentence in which the word appears, to determine the word's meaning. Write your definition here and identify clues that helped you figure out its meaning.

Skill:
Technical Language

Use the Checklist to analyze Technical Language in "Machines, not people, should be exploring the stars for now." Refer to the sample student annotations about Technical Language in the text.

••• CHECKLIST FOR TECHNICAL LANGUAGE

In order to determine the meanings of words and phrases as they are used in a text, note the following:

- ✓ the subject of the book or article

- ✓ any unfamiliar words that you think might be technical terms

- ✓ words that have multiple meanings that change when used with a specific subject

- ✓ the possible contextual meaning of a word, or the definition from a dictionary

To determine the meanings of words and phrases as they are used in a text, including technical meanings, consider the following questions:

- ✓ What is the subject of the informational text?

- ✓ How does the use of technical language help establish the author as an authority on the subject?

- ✓ Are there any technical words that have an impact on the meaning and tone, or quality, of the book or article?

- ✓ Can you identify the contextual meaning of any of the words?

Please note that excerpts and passages in the StudySync® library and this workbook are intended as touchstones to generate interest in an author's work. The excerpts and passages do not substitute for the reading of entire texts, and StudySync® strongly recommends that students seek out and purchase the whole literary or informational work in order to experience it as the author intended. Links to online resellers are available in our digital library. In addition, complete works may be ordered through an authorized reseller by filling out and returning to StudySync® the order form enclosed in this workbook.

Reading & Writing Companion   73

Skill:
Technical Language

Reread paragraphs 13–14 of "Machines, not people, should be exploring the stars for now." Then, using the Checklist on the previous page, answer the multiple-choice questions below.

⟳ YOUR TURN

1. This question has two parts. First, answer Part A. Then, answer Part B.

   Part A: Which sentence below contains multiple technical terms specific to space exploration?

   ○ A. There are three important goals we need to achieve.

   ○ B. The first is monitoring our own world, resulting in storm warnings and help in understanding our complex planet.

   ○ C. But it's not just about the money.

   ○ D. Robotic exploration, through either space probes or telescopes, provides a much better yield for much lower money.

   Part B: What is the effect of the technical terms in Part A?

   ○ A. It helps the tone sounds light and friendly.

   ○ B. It makes the author sound educated and believable.

   ○ C. It makes the author sound like he is trying too hard.

   ○ D. It makes the reader wonder if the author knows what he's talking about.

Skill: Greek and Latin Affixes and Roots

Use the Checklist to analyze Greek and Latin Affixes and Roots in "Machines, not people, should be exploring the stars for now." Refer to the sample student annotations about Greek and Latin Affixes and Roots in the text.

••• CHECKLIST FOR GREEK AND LATIN AFFIXES AND ROOTS

In order to identify Greek and Latin affixes and roots, note the following:

✓ the root

✓ the prefix and/or suffix

To use common, grade-appropriate Greek or Latin affixes and roots as clues to the meaning of a word, use the following questions as a guide:

✓ Can I identify the root of this word? Should I look in a dictionary or other resource?

✓ What is the meaning of the root?

✓ Can I identify the prefix and/or suffix of this word? Should I look in a dictionary or other resource?

✓ What is the meaning of the prefix and/or suffix?

✓ Does this suffix change the word's part of speech?

✓ How do the word parts work together to determine the word's meaning and part of speech?

Please note that excerpts and passages in the StudySync® library and this workbook are intended as touchstones to generate interest in an author's work. The excerpts and passages do not substitute for the reading of entire texts, and StudySync® strongly recommends that students seek out and purchase the whole literary or informational work in order to experience it as the author intended. Links to online resellers are available in our digital library. In addition, complete works may be ordered through an authorized reseller by filling out and returning to StudySync® the order form enclosed in this workbook.

Reading & Writing Companion   75

Skill: Greek and Latin Affixes and Roots

Reread paragraph 12 from "Machines, not people, should be exploring the stars for now." Then, using the Checklist on the previous page as well as the dictionary entries below, answer the multiple-choice questions.

↻ YOUR TURN

cosmos cos•mos \'koz-məs\ or \kos-mōs\
origin: from the Greek *kosmos* meaning "order, good order, orderly arrangement"

telescope tel•e•scope \'tel-ə-'skōp\
origin: from the Greek *tele-* meaning "far" + *skopos* meaning "watcher"

discovery dis•cov•er•y \dis 'kəv-ə-rē\
origin: from the Latin *dis-* meaning "opposite of" + *cooperire* meaning "to cover up" + *y*, a noun suffix

1. Based on its context and root, what is the most likely meaning of *cosmos*?

   ○ A. an orderly way of doing something
   ○ B. a good guess or approximation
   ○ C. a well-ordered universe
   ○ D. a mysterious and hard-to-reach place

2. Based on its context and root, what is the most likely meaning of *telescope*?

   ○ A. a device that lets you view objects at far distances
   ○ B. a very expensive scientific instrument
   ○ C. an invention that helps you track objects as they move
   ○ D. a gadget that reproduces images in a laboratory

3. Based on its context, suffix, and root, what is the most likely meaning of *discovery*?

   ○ A. in a new or unusual way
   ○ B. the process of hiding something
   ○ C. to become aware of something
   ○ D. the act of finding something

Skill:
Reasons and Evidence

Use the Checklist to analyze Reasons and Evidence in "Machines, not people, should be exploring the stars for now." Refer to the sample student annotations about Reasons and Evidence in the text.

••• CHECKLIST FOR REASONS AND EVIDENCE

In order to identify the reasons and evidence that support an author's claim(s) in an argument, note the following:

- ✓ the argument the author is making

- ✓ the claim or the main idea of the argument

- ✓ the reasons and evidence that support the claim and where they can be found

- ✓ if the evidence the author presents to support the claim is sound, or complete and comprehensive

- ✓ if there is sufficient evidence to support the claim or if more is needed

To assess whether the author's reasoning is sound and the evidence is relevant and sufficient, consider the following questions:

- ✓ What kind of argument is the author making?

- ✓ Is the reasoning, or the thinking behind the claims, sound and valid?

- ✓ Are the reasons and evidence the author presents to support the claim sufficient, or is more evidence needed? Why or why not?

Please note that excerpts and passages in the StudySync® library and this workbook are intended as touchstones to generate interest in an author's work. The excerpts and passages do not substitute for the reading of entire texts, and StudySync® strongly recommends that students seek out and purchase the whole literary or informational work in order to experience it as the author intended. Links to online resellers are available in our digital library. In addition, complete works may be ordered through an authorized reseller by filling out and returning to StudySync® the order form enclosed in this workbook.

Reading & Writing
Companion

77

Skill:
Reasons and Evidence

Reread paragraphs 11–12 of "Machines, not people, should be exploring the stars for now." Then, using the Checklist on the previous page, answer the multiple-choice questions below.

♺ YOUR TURN

1. This question has two parts. First, answer Part A. Then, answer Part B.

   Part A: In paragraph 11, Lincoln claims that robotic space exploration is less expensive than manned space flight. How does he support this claim?

   ○ A. Expert opinions

   ○ B. Quotes

   ○ C. Numerical evidence

   ○ D. Statistics

   Part B: What piece of evidence best supports your answer to Part A?

   ○ A. The Cassini mission to Saturn cost about $3.2 billion. The Mars Curiosity Rover cost about $2.5 billion.

   ○ B. In contrast, robotic exploration of the solar system is far less costly.

   ○ C. Mars missions have explored ancient streams where knee-deep water once flowed and have found organic carbon embedded in surface rocks.

   ○ D. These and other missions have been wildly successful in teaching us about places where literally no one has gone before.

Close Read

Reread "Machines, not people, should be exploring the stars for now." As you reread, complete the Skills Focus questions below. Then use your answers and annotations from the questions to help you complete the Write activity.

◎ SKILLS FOCUS

1. Recall that an author's purpose is his or her reason for writing. Identify a detail that reveals the author's purpose, and explain how he works toward achieving that purpose.

2. Recall that an author uses claims to support his or her argument. Identify two or three claims Don Lincoln uses to support his argument that using robots is the best way to explore space.

3. The text deals with a scientific topic and uses the technical language associated with the field. Identify phrases with technical language, and write a note explaining the impact of that language.

4. Choose one claim that Lincoln uses to support his argument. Explain and assess whether Lincoln's evidence is relevant and sufficient to support the claim.

5. The author and people with an opposing opinion disagree about how to explore space, but they share the same dream. Identify details that tell what that dream is, and explain what makes the dream worth pursuing.

✏ WRITE

INFORMATIVE: Imagine that you are writing a flyer to gain support for America to invest in space technology and exploration. Which points from the article would you include in the flyer to persuade your readers? Write the text for this flyer, using information from the article and, if necessary, research other sources. Use technical language, and include a claim with reasons and evidence to show your audience your stance.

Please note that excerpts and passages in the StudySync® library and this workbook are intended as touchstones to generate interest in an author's work. The excerpts and passages do not substitute for the reading of entire texts, and StudySync® strongly recommends that students seek out and purchase the whole literary or informational work in order to experience it as the author intended. Links to online resellers are available in our digital library. In addition, complete works may be ordered through an authorized reseller by filling out and returning to StudySync® the order form enclosed in this workbook.

Reading & Writing Companion **79**

Responses to "Machines, not people, should be exploring the stars for now"

ARGUMENTATIVE TEXT
StudySync
2017

Introduction

In "Machines, not people, should be exploring the stars for now," American physicist Don Lincoln argues that it would be more beneficial to shift our focus to robotic space travel—for now, at least. He takes into consideration both costs and human versus robotic ability to withstand other environments. Although much of space exploration is currently focused on manned space travel, Lincoln concludes that robots should first find habitable planets before manned missions are undertaken. Following are six different reader responses that agree or disagree with the author's points.

"Why should we spend so much to take a risk we do not yet need to take?"

NOTES

Manned Space Exploration Makes Money Too

1   Your concerns about the costs of space exploration are valid. However, you miss an important benefit of these costs, Mr. Lincoln. You did not mention how often space exploration actually creates unexpected value for both the government and businesses. Meeting the challenge of sustaining fragile humans in inhospitable environments requires **innovation**. The Apollo program alone has led to many innovations. They include new athletic shoes, solar panels, heart monitors, pacemakers,[1] and cordless tools. Both the U.S. government and businesses have been able to patent and **generate revenue** from these inventions. These profits may not equal the billions the government must invest in a particular space program, but they are important investments in the country's **economy**.

Isabel Flores
San Jose, CA

A Practical Plan for Space Exploration

2   This plan for future space exploration seems very practical. Space exploration is costly. It makes sense to use a cheaper method for now. Robot missions can determine whether a planet is even worth exploring before committing more resources. Manned programs can cost tens or hundreds of times more than robotic ones. Using robots helps scientists use their resources more wisely. They can

Curiosity is an unmanned rover that was designed to explore Mars as part of NASA's Mars Science Laboratory mission. *Curiosity* was launched from Cape Canaveral on November 26, 2011, and landed on Mars on August 6, 2012.

---

1. **pacemakers** electrical devices placed close to the heart to regulate arrhythmia, or irregular heartbeats

NOTES

carry out initial explorations of more places, increasing the chances of making an important discovery.

Joon Kim
Ridgefield, NJ

We Should be Brave and Fearless

3   Our country has a long tradition of exploration. The daring achievements of explorers have made the United States a powerful nation. But now America is losing its position at the top. In order to remain a global leader, a nation must be brave, fearless, and willing to take risks. That means America needs to continue to lead the way in space exploration with human astronauts. Men and women traveling into space commands respect and admiration, both nationally and internationally. Are we going to risk our position in the world because we are too cowardly to send humans into space? The only way for our country to advance is to proceed with bravery and fearlessness, and that means sending American men and women, not robots, to explore space.

Nora Jensen
Greenfield, IA

Space Exploration in Perspective

4   I think Mr. Lincoln is correct in **prioritizing** cheaper, unmanned space missions over manned space exploration. This is especially important for government programs like NASA. Limiting the cost of space exploration would allow the U.S. government to invest more money in programs with more urgent need. That money could be used to provide better services to veterans or create more affordable housing. Why should the government invest billions of dollars in a program with no real urgency? Why should we spend so much to take a risk we do not yet need to take? Space exploration is important. But our investment in the future should not be prioritized over addressing the real challenges we face today.

Sylvia Johnson
Washington, D.C.

Inspiring Innovation

5 Mr. Lincoln forgets the symbolic importance of manned space programs. They drive innovation not just out of necessity, but also through inspiration. The Apollo missions encouraged many people to seek careers in the sciences. Some became astronauts. Others sought careers in related fields. The ability of humans to make progress in space exploration helps people believe in their own **potential**. Unmanned space exploration does not have the same symbolic effect.

This command capsule, built by North American Rockwell's Space Division for use in human-led space flight, was launched in October 1968 in NASA's first successful Apollo mission. Here, engineers and technicians check the capsule before its departure for Cape Kennedy.

Michael Williams
Houston, TX

Not Worth Dying For

6 Mr. Lincoln rightfully reminds us of the risks involved in sending humans to explore space. Every time we launch a spacecraft with astronauts aboard we put their lives in danger, and too many astronauts have died already. Space exploration is important, but protecting and preserving human life should always be the priority. Unmanned space exploration can complete tasks more efficiently and without the risk of losing human life. It is not only foolish and misguided but downright cruel to keep sending astronauts to their deaths. People in favor of sending humans into space—when we could more safely and effectively send robots instead—have no regard for human life.

Mark Scarborough
Weatherford, TX

RESPONSES TO "MACHINES, NOT PEOPLE, SHOULD BE EXPLORING THE STARS FOR NOW"

First Read

Read "Responses to 'Machines, not people, should be exploring the stars for now.'" After you read, complete the Think Questions below.

☁ THINK QUESTIONS

1. What is the most important idea of response 2? Provide specific examples from the text to support your answer.

2. Why does the author of response 4 agree that it would be better to use less costly robots in space exploration? What does she say the money saved could be used for instead? Cite two specific examples from the text.

3. What is the main reason Mark Scarborough agrees with Lincoln's article? Use textual evidence to support your answer.

4. Find the word **prioritizing** in response 4. Use context clues in the surrounding sentences, as well as the sentence in which the word appears, to determine the word's meaning. Write your definition here and identify clues that helped you figure out the meaning.

5. Use context clues to determine the meaning of the word **potential** as it is used in response 5. Write your own definition of *potential* and identify clues that helped you figure out the meaning. Then check a dictionary to confirm the definition.

Skill:
Compare and Contrast

Use the Checklist to analyze Compare and Contrast in "Responses to 'Machines, not people, should be exploring the stars for now.'" Refer to the sample student annotations about Compare and Contrast in the text.

••• CHECKLIST FOR COMPARE AND CONTRAST

In order to determine how two or more authors writing about the same topic shape their presentations of key information, use the following steps:

✓ First, choose two texts with similar subjects or topics by different authors.

✓ Next, identify each author's approach to the subject.

✓ After, identify the key information and evidence that each author includes.

✓ Then, explain the ways each author shapes his or her presentation of the information in the text.

✓ Finally, analyze the similarities and differences in how the authors present:

• key information

• evidence

• their interpretation of facts

To analyze how two or more authors writing about the same topic shape their presentations of key information, consider the following questions:

✓ In what ways do the texts I have chosen have similar subjects or topics?

✓ How does each author approach the topic or subject?

✓ How does each author's presentation of key information differ? How are the presentations the same? How do these similarities and differences change the presentation and interpretation of the facts?

COMPARE AND CONTRAST
sync•skills

Skill:
Compare and Contrast

Reread the following responses: "A Practical Plan for Space Exploration," "Space Exploration in Perspective," and "Not Worth Dying For." Then match the summary to the appropriate text in the chart below.

⟳ YOUR TURN

	Summary
A	Manned space travel is too dangerous, and sending robots helps keep people safe.
B	There are more important things for the government to spend money on than manned space travel.
C	Robotic space exploration is cheaper and more practical.

Common Argument: The bad aspects of manned space travel outweigh the good aspects.

"A Practical Plan for Space Exploration"	"Space Exploration in Perspective"	"Not Worth Dying For"

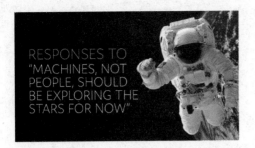

Close Read

Reread "Responses to 'Machines, not people, should be exploring the stars for now.'" As you reread, complete the Skills Focus questions below. Then use your answers and annotations from the questions to help you complete the Write activity.

◎ SKILLS FOCUS

1. Identify different types of evidence in the responses. Write a note explaining whether the evidence provides adequate support for the author's claim.

2. Which of the authors' claims are supported by sufficient evidence and sound reasons? Which are not supported? Highlight claims, and write a note about how the author supports his or her claims.

3. Compare and contrast the different authors' arguments. Identify pertinent examples and supporting evidence the authors use. Write a note explaining how the examples and evidence support their arguments and claims.

4. Choose two responses that you agree with. For each, identify a statement that indicates the author's purpose in writing a response. Then explain how the statement supports the author's purpose.

5. In the fifth response, identify details that show why the dream of human space exploration is worth pursuing. Then explain how these details develop the author's main argument.

✎ WRITE

DISCUSSION: In this informational text, a series of people respond to an argument about how America should invest its money in space exploration. Pretend you are a member of the Congressional budget committee, which helps decide how to spend America's money, and debate the issue with your classmates. Should the government spend money on manned missions to space, or should they focus on robotic missions? Discuss this question with a group of your peers. To prepare for your discussion, use a graphic organizer to write down your ideas about the prompt. Support your ideas with evidence from the text. You may also reference Don Lincoln's original essay. After your discussion, you will write a reflection.

Extended Writing Project and Grammar

EXTENDED WRITING PROJECT

ARGUMENTATIVE WRITING

Argumentative Writing Process: Plan

| PLAN | DRAFT | REVISE | EDIT AND PUBLISH |

In this unit, you have read and learned about people chasing dreams that seem impossible to them. Sometimes, that dream is a common one, like a college education. In other cases, the dream captures our imaginations and requires major planning to achieve, like space exploration. In all of those cases, the person pursuing that dream knew why it was worth pursuing and worked to gather the information he or she needed to pursue it.

WRITING PROMPT

What are your interests, goals, and dreams? What club, class, or activity would you add to your school to help you achieve these goals or dreams?

Your principal has announced an essay writing contest:

If you had the option of adding a club, a class, or an activity to your school, what would it be and why would it be worth including? Think about why you would like it added to your school's offerings. Why is this club, class, or activity important to the school? How would other students benefit from this addition? Write an argumentative essay to convince your teachers or school leaders to establish this new club, class, or activity. In your essay, present your argument, with clear reasons and relevant evidence. Be sure your essay includes the following:

- an introduction
- a thesis statement with claims
- coherent body paragraphs
- reasons and evidence
- a conclusion

Introduction to Argumentative Writing

An argumentative essay is a form of persuasive writing where the writer makes a claim about a topic and then provides evidence—facts, details, examples, and quotations—to convince readers to accept and agree with the writer's claim. In order to provide convincing supporting evidence for an argumentative essay, the writer must often do outside research as well as cite the sources of the evidence that is presented in the essay.

The characteristics of argumentative writing include:

- introduction
- thesis statement with claims
- reasons and evidence
- transitions
- formal style
- conclusion

As you continue with this Extended Writing Project, you'll receive more instruction and practice in crafting each of the characteristics of argumentative writing to create your own argumentative essay.

Before you get started on your own essay, read this essay that one student, Cameron, wrote in response to the writing prompt. As you read the Model, highlight and annotate the features of argumentative writing that Cameron included in her essay.

≡ STUDENT MODEL

NOTES

The Case for Makerspace

1   Have you ever built or created something on your own? How amazing would it have been to be able to do that in school! One way to do this is to build a makerspace at North End School. A makerspace is a place where students will be able to use technology to design, experiment, and invent through hands-on practice. Some might argue that we should add more athletic resources or art programs, but a makerspace is one of the only additions to our school that could be used by almost every class: science, math, art, and even English class! Overall, we should add a makerspace to North End School because it's a place to create and do experiments, it will help prepare students for the STEM jobs of the future, and it is a big opportunity for teachers too.

2   Makerspaces are inspiring places where people can learn to create and invent with confidence. Students will learn new skills, boost creativity, and build self-esteem by making things. For example, students can design everything from physics experiments to jewelry. A recent report from the New Media Consortium says, "Schools are turning to makerspaces to facilitate activities that inspire confidence in young learners." Having a makerspace for art or design will help students be confident and well-rounded. This is important because students will be happier and be able to achieve their dreams to be designers, artists, or engineers.

3   A makerspace at our school can help other students at North End pursue interests that can lead to great futures—something we all want. According to the U.S. Bureau of Labor Statistics, jobs in science, technology, engineering, and mathematics (STEM) are increasing by about 1 million from 2012 to 2022. Since the industry is experiencing a growth spurt, the time to act is now. A makerspace would give students an opportunity to learn about new technology with hands-on experience. Our 7th-grade class may have a number of future stars

NOTES

in new technology, but without a makerspace, we might not reach our potential. Imagine feeling like we left this class behind at a critical turning point. We need a makerspace to be ready for the jobs of the future.

4   In addition to preparing students for the future, North End teachers also think a makerspace would benefit the school and students right now. Because a makerspace can be used in many ways, teachers in multiple subjects could use a makerspace for special projects in science, art, and math, and they could also use it for an after-school club. Before last semester ended, interviews were conducted with several teachers at North End. The technology teacher, Mr. Smith, said that a makerspace would "provide students with the opportunity for a powerful experience to enhance their thinking." Ms. Bo, the 7th-grade science teacher, said that "the addition of a makerspace and its equipment would foster creativity, tinkering, and curiosity, which leads to better thinking and better questioning." This clearly shows that teachers think a makerspace would improve the quality of their classes and student thinking.

5   North End School would greatly benefit from a makerspace for three main reasons. Building a makerspace in our school would create a way for students to develop creative skills that would help them in their futures. It would give them a chance to explore new passions and industries. The goal of our studies at school is to help us reach our potential, and research in the fields of STEM and conversations with our own teachers show that the addition of a makerspace to our school would help make our school better.

WRITE

Writers often take notes before they sit down to write. Think about what you've learned so far about argumentative writing to help you begin prewriting.

- What club, class, or activity would you like to add to your school?

- How would this club, class, or activity benefit other students? Why is it worthwhile? List a few reasons.

- Who is your audience and what message do you want to express to your audience?

Response Instructions

Use the questions in the bulleted list to write a one-paragraph summary. Your summary should explain what your essay will be about, including why it will be worthwhile. Don't worry about including all of the details now; focus only on the most essential and important elements in the bulleted list. You will refer back to this short paragraph as you continue through the steps of the writing process.

Skill:
Thesis Statement

••• CHECKLIST FOR THESIS STATEMENT

Before you begin writing your thesis statement, ask yourself the following questions:

- What is the prompt asking me to write about?

- What is the topic of my essay? How can I state it clearly for the reader?

- What claim(s) do I want to make about the topic of this essay? Is my opinion clear to my reader?

Here are some methods to introduce and develop your claim and topic clearly:

- Think about the topic and central idea of your essay.

  > Is the central idea of an argument stated?

  > Have you identified as many claims as you intend to prove?

- Write a clear statement about the central idea or claim(s). Your thesis statement should:

  > let the reader anticipate the body of your essay

  > respond completely to the prompt

YOUR TURN

Read the following notes made by Cameron's classmate while he was drafting his thesis statement. Then, complete the chart by writing the corresponding letter for each note in the correct place in the outline.

Note Options	
A	We currently have more students who would like to participate in team sports than the number of teams we have.
B	Establish a pickleball club at North End School.
C	One way to improve North End School is to establish a pickleball club because we currently have more students than teams and pickleball is a growing sport that would be a great addition to school.
D	Pickleball is a growing sport that would be a great addition to student life at our school.

Outline	Note
School Addition:	
Claim 1:	
Claim 2:	
Thesis Statement:	

WRITE

Follow the steps in the checklist section to draft a thesis statement for your argumentative essay.

Skill: Organizing Argumentative Writing

••• CHECKLIST FOR ORGANIZING ARGUMENTATIVE WRITING

As you consider how to organize your writing for your argumentative essay, use the following questions as a guide:

- What is my position on this topic?

- Have I chosen the best organizational structure to present my information logically?

- Can my claim be supported by logical reasoning and relevant evidence?

- Do I have enough evidence to support my claim or thesis?

- How can I organize the reasons and evidence clearly?

- How can I clarify the relationships between my claims and reasons?

Follow these steps to plan out the organization of your argumentative essay, including organizing your reasons and evidence logically:

- Identify and write your thesis.

- Choose an organizational structure that will present your claims logically and clearly.

- Identify reasons and evidence that support each claim.

- Organize your ideas using an outline or graphic organizer.

⟳ YOUR TURN

Imagine a student is just beginning her outline to argue for the addition of a photography studio to her school. Read the statements below. Then, complete the chart by writing the corresponding letter for each statement in the correct place in the outline.

	Statement Options
A	The first reason is that art students would be able to get more practice in the medium of photography.
B	In conclusion, adding a photography studio would improve our school because more students would practice photography, learn about photojournalism, and participate in clubs.
C	A photography studio would be an amazing addition to the art program at North End School because more students would practice photography, learn about photojournalism, and join after-school clubs.
D	The third reason for a photography studio is that it would get more students involved through after-school clubs.
E	Journalism students would be able to learn more about photojournalism.

Outline	Statement
Thesis Statement:	
Claim 1:	
Claim 2:	
Claim 3:	
Repeat Thesis Statement:	

YOUR TURN

Complete the chart below by writing a short summary of what you will focus on in each paragraph of your essay.

Outline	Statement
Thesis Statement:	
Claim 1:	
Claim 2:	
Claim 3:	
Repeat Thesis Statement:	

Skill: Reasons and Relevant Evidence

••• **CHECKLIST FOR REASONS AND RELEVANT EVIDENCE**

As you begin to determine what reasons and relevant evidence will support your claim(s), use the following questions as a guide:

- What is the claim (or claims) that I am making in my argument?

- What textual evidence am I using to support this claim? Is it relevant?

- Am I quoting the source accurately?

- Does my evidence display logical reasoning and relate to the claim I am making?

- How can I demonstrate my understanding of the topic or source material?

Use the following steps as a guide to help you determine how you will support your claim(s) with logical reasoning and relevant, sufficient evidence, using accurate and credible sources:

- Identify the claim(s) you will make in your argument.

- Select sufficient evidence from credible sources that will convince others to accept your claim(s).

- Explain the connection between your claim(s) and the evidence and ensure your reasoning is logical, develops naturally from the evidence, and supports your claim.

YOUR TURN

Read each claim in the chart below. Then, complete the chart by matching the evidence with the claim it best supports and explaining how the evidence sufficiently supports that claim. The first row has been done for you.

	Evidence Options
A	Statistics show that cell phone use while driving causes 1.6 million crashes each year, and nearly one out of every four accidents is caused by texting and driving.
B	Surveys show that 65% of cell phone owners say that their phones have made it a lot easier to stay in touch with the people they care about.
C	Since 1970, the number of fast food restaurants in business has doubled. At the same time, the percentage of the U.S. population suffering from obesity has increased from about 15% to nearly 40% of the population.
D	Less than 5% of adults participate in at least 30 minutes of physical activity every day, and only one in three receive the recommended amount of physical activity each week.

Claim	Evidence	Reasoning
Fast food is contributing to the obesity epidemic.	C	This supports the idea that as the number of fast food restaurants has increased, so has the obesity level.
Americans are also unhealthy because they do not exercise enough.		
Texting while driving is unsafe.		
Cell phones have made positive impacts on our lives.		

↻ YOUR TURN

List three claims from your essay. Then, complete the chart by writing a piece of evidence that supports each of your claims and explain how this evidence sufficiently supports the claim.

Claim	Evidence	Reasoning
Claim 1:		
Claim 2:		
Claim 3:		

Please note that excerpts and passages in the StudySync® library and this workbook are intended as touchstones to generate interest in an author's work. The excerpts and passages do not substitute for the reading of entire texts, and StudySync® strongly recommends that students seek out and purchase the whole literary or informational work in order to experience it as the author intended. Links to online resellers are available in our digital library. In addition, complete works may be ordered through an authorized reseller by filling out and returning to StudySync® the order form enclosed in this workbook.

Reading & Writing
Companion

101

Argumentative Writing Process: Draft

PLAN	DRAFT	REVISE	EDIT AND PUBLISH

You have already made progress toward writing your essay. Now it is time to draft your argumentative essay.

✏ WRITE

Use your plan and other responses in your Binder to draft your essay. You may also have new ideas as you begin drafting. Feel free to explore those new ideas as you have them. You can also ask yourself these questions:

- Have I written my thesis statement clearly?

- Is my textual evidence relevant and necessary?

- Does the organizational structure make sense?

Before you submit your draft, read it over carefully. You want to be sure that you've responded to all aspects of the prompt.

Here is Cameron's essay draft. As you read, identify relevant textual evidence that develops the thesis statement and claims. As Cameron continues to revise and edit her essay, she will find and improve weak spots in her writing, as well as correct any language or punctuation mistakes.

☰ STUDENT MODEL: FIRST DRAFT

The Case for Makerspace

~~I believe our school would benefit from a makerspace. Makerspaces are hubs of activity where people can do many things using a range of technology. We should add a makerspace to North End School because it's a place to create and do experiments, it will help prepare students for jobs in science, and it is a big opportunity for teachers too.~~

Have you ever built or created something on your own? How amazing would it have been to be able to do that in school! One way to do this is to build a makerspace at North End School. A makerspace is a place where students will be able to use technology to design, experiment, and invent through hands-on practice. Some might argue that we should add more athletic resources or art programs, but a makerspace is one of the only additions to our school that could be used by almost every class: science, math, art, and even English class! Overall, we should add a makerspace to North End School because it's a place to create and do experiments, it will help prepare students for the STEM jobs of the future, and it is a big opportunity for teachers too.

~~Makerspaces are a place to create and do experiments. Students will learn new skills, boost creativity, and self-esteem by making things. Students can design everything from physics experiments to jewelry. A recent report from the New Media Consortium says, "Schools are turning to makerspaces to facilitate activities that inspire confidence in young learners." Having a makerspace for art or design will help students be confident and well-rounded. Students will be happier and be able to achieve dreams to be designers, artists, or engineers.~~

Makerspaces are inspiring places where people can learn to create and invent with confidence. Students will learn new skills, boost

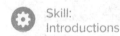

Skill:
Introductions

Cameron revised her introductory paragraph. She added a question and a follow-up sentence to hook her reader's attention. Then she acknowledged opposing claims and used them to strengthen her argument.

Skill:
Transitions

Cameron decides to add a stronger topic sentence that will help her connect her paragraph to the rest of the essay. She also realizes that there was a sudden jump in her ideas, especially when she began talking about student dreams. She decides to revise the paragraph to create cohesion between it and the rest of her essay.

Skill:
Style

Cameron revised this paragraph of her essay so that she established a formal academic tone. She changed instances of the first person (I and we) to third-person pronouns. Cameron noticed that her tone was very conversational in her draft, so she revised it to be more formal and used her teachers' names and titles to help persuade her readers.

creativity, and build self-esteem by making things. For example, students can design everything from physics experiments to jewelry. A recent report from the New Media Consortium says, "Schools are turning to makerspaces to facilitate activities that inspire confidence in young learners." Having a makerspace for art or design will help students be confident and well-rounded. This is important because students will be happier and be able to achieve their dreams to be designers, artists, or engineers.

A makerspace at our school can help other students at North End follow interests that can lead to great futures—something we all want. According to the U.S. Bureau of Labor Statistics, jobs in science, technology, engineering, and mathematics (STEM) are increasing by about 1 million from 2012 to 2022. Since the industry is experiencing a growth spurt, the time to act is now. A makerspace would give students an opportunity to learn about new technology with hands-on experience. Our 7th-grade class may have a number of future stars in new technology, but without a makerspace, we might not reach our potential. Imagine feeling like we left this class behind at a critical turning point. We need a makerspace to be ready for the jobs of the future.

~~I think that lots of teachers at North End agree with me. As a school community, we should make sure our students get the very best. Mr. Smith and some other teachers all did interviews that they all think it's a great idea. The tech and 7th-grade scince teacher think the makerspace and its equippment would help students and their thinking. I bet we could even use it for an after school club!~~

In addition to preparing students for the future, North End teachers also think a makerspace would benefit the school and students right now. Because a makerspace can be used in many ways, teachers in multiple subjects could use a makerspace for special projects in science, art, and math, and they could also use it for an after-school club. Before last semester ended, interviews were conducted with several teachers at North End. The technology teacher, Mr. Smith, said that a makerspace would "provide students with the opportunity for a powerful experience to enhance their thinking." Ms. Bo, the 7th-grade science teacher, said that "the addition of a makerspace and its equipment would foster creativity, tinkering, and curiosity, which leads to better thinking and better questioning." This clearly shows that teachers think a makerspace would improve the quality of their classes and student thinking.

A makerspace is the best addition for our school. It would help students in lots of different ways and make our school better.

North End School would greatly benefit from a makerspace for three main reasons. Building a makerspace in our school would create a way for students to develop creative skills that would help them in their futures. It would give them a chance to explore new passions and industries. The goal of our studies at school is to help us reach our potential, and research in the fields of STEM and conversations with our own teachers show that the addition of a makerspace to our school would help make our school better.

NOTES

Skill:
Conclusions

Cameron made her conclusion stronger by restating her thesis at the beginning of the paragraph and then briefly reviewing the claims and some of the evidence that supported them. She ended with a memorable comment, connecting her argument about a makerspace to the bigger goals of education and how a makerspace would help achieve those goals.

Please note that excerpts and passages in the StudySync® library and this workbook are intended as touchstones to generate interest in an author's work. The excerpts and passages do not substitute for the reading of entire texts, and StudySync® strongly recommends that students seek out and purchase the whole literary or informational work in order to experience it as the author intended. Links to online resellers are available in our digital library. In addition, complete works may be ordered through an authorized reseller by filling out and returning to StudySync® the order form enclosed in this workbook.

Reading & Writing Companion

105

Skill:
Introductions

••• CHECKLIST FOR INTRODUCTIONS

Before you write your introduction, ask yourself the following questions:

- How will I "hook" my reader's interest? You might:

  > start with an attention-grabbing statement

  > begin with an intriguing question

- Have I introduced my topic clearly?

- What is my argument and claim(s)? Have I recognized opposing claims that disagree with mine or use a different perspective? How can I use them to strengthen my own?

- Where should I place my thesis statement? You might:

  > put your thesis statement at the end of your introduction to help readers preview your body paragraphs

Below are two strategies to help you introduce your claim and topic clearly in an introduction:

- Peer Discussion

  > Talk about your topic with a partner, explaining what you already know and your ideas about your topic.

  > Write notes about the ideas you have discussed and any new questions you may have.

- Freewriting

  > Freewrite for ten minutes about your topic. Don't worry about grammar, punctuation, or having fully formed ideas. The point of freewriting is to discover ideas.

  > Review your notes and think about what your claim or controlling idea will be.

YOUR TURN

Read the sentences below, taken from the introduction Cameron's friend wrote. Then, complete the chart by placing each sentence in its correct place in the introduction outline.

	Sentence Options
A	Some might argue that our school should focus on adding more academic programs; however, dance can help students who are struggling find an outlet and express themselves positively.
B	One way to improve North End School would be to add a dance club.
C	Don't you think that school should encourage students to follow their dreams and passions?
D	Adding a dance club to North End School would be beneficial for many different kinds of students and is the best thing that we can add to our school.

Introduction Outline	Sentence
Hook	
Introduce the topic & argument	
Recognize opposing claims	
Thesis statement	

✏ WRITE

Use the steps in the checklist section to revise the introduction of your argumentative essay.

Skill:
Transitions

Copyright © BookheadEd Learning, LLC

••• CHECKLIST FOR TRANSITIONS

Before you revise your current draft to include transitions, think about:

- the key ideas you discuss in your body paragraphs

- how your paragraphs connect together to support your claim(s)

- the relationships among your claim(s), reasons, and evidence

Next, reread your current draft and note areas in your essay where:

- the relationships between your claim(s) and the reasons and evidence are unclear, identifying places where you could add linking words or other transitional devices to make your argument more cohesive. Look for:

  > sudden jumps in your ideas

  > breaks between paragraphs where the ideas in the next paragraph are not logically following from the previous one

Revise your draft to use words, phrases, and clauses to create cohesion and clarify the relationships among claim(s) and reasons, using the following questions as a guide:

  > Are there unifying relationships between the claims, reasons, and evidence I present in my argument?

  > Have I clarified, or made clear, these relationships?

↻ YOUR TURN

Choose the best answer to each question.

1. Below is a section from a previous draft of Cameron's essay. Cameron has not used an effective transition in the underlined sentence. Which of the following could she add to the underlined sentence?

> This is important because many students have dreams to be designers, artists, and engineers. <u>I have dreams of becoming a shoe designer or an engineer one day.</u>

- ○ A. Similarly,
- ○ B. For example,
- ○ C. Equally important,
- ○ D. However,

2. The following section is from an earlier draft of Cameron's essay. She would like to add a sentence to bring this paragraph to a close more effectively. Which sentence could she add after sentence 4 to achieve this goal?

> (1) A makerspace at our school can help other students at North End pursue interests that can lead to great futures—something we all want. (2) According to the U.S. Bureau of Labor Statistics, jobs in STEM are increasing by about 1 million from 2012 to 2022. (3) The time to act is now. (4) Our 7th-grade class may have a number of future stars in new technology, but without a makerspace, we might not reach our potential.

- ○ A. It would help us grow our art and technology programs.
- ○ B. A survey of students indicated that a makerspace is one of the most popular additions.
- ○ C. In conclusion, by adding one, we may help students here live up to their full potential.
- ○ D. For example, including a makerspace might help more students become interested in science and technology.

YOUR TURN

Complete the chart by writing a transitional sentence that connects ideas and creates cohesion between paragraphs in your essay.

Purpose	Example	Your Transitional Sentence
add information	**In addition,** it is important to remember athletic programs help students develop social and leadership skills.	
discuss a contradiction	**Even though** another art or music program would be nice, creating more athletic programming for our girls is necessary for things to be equal.	
introduce examples	**For example,** the math and science scores at West Side High School increased by 34% when additional art and music programs were added.	
show time sequence	**At the present time,** there are two teachers who already support this addition.	
summarize	**In summary,** I believe that a new technology club would be the best addition to our school.	

Skill: Style

••• CHECKLIST FOR STYLE

First, reread the draft of your argumentative essay and identify the following:

- places where you use slang, contractions, abbreviations, and a conversational tone

- areas where you could use subject-specific or academic language in order to help persuade or inform your readers

- moments where you use the first person (*I*) or second person (*you*)

- areas where your sentence structure lacks variety

- incorrect uses of the conventions of standard English for grammar, spelling, capitalization, and punctuation

Establish and maintain a formal style in your essay, using the following questions as a guide:

- Have I avoided slang in favor of academic language?

- Did I consistently use a third-person point of view, using third-person pronouns (*he, she, they*)?

- Have I varied my sentence structure and the length of my sentences? Ask yourself these specific questions:

  > Where should I make some sentences longer by using conjunctions to connect independent clauses, dependent clauses, and phrases?

  > Where should I make some sentences shorter by separating any independent clauses?

- Did I follow the conventions of standard English, including:

  > grammar?

  > spelling?

  > capitalization?

  > punctuation?

↻ YOUR TURN

Read the sentences showing an informal and formal style below. Then, complete the chart by writing the informal language option that correctly describes each type of informal language that was revised to a formal style.

Informal Language Options	
A	Conversational Tone
B	Contractions
C	First Person
D	Slang

Informal Style	Type of Informal Language	Revised to a Formal Style
They didn't realize how important it was.		They did not realize how important it was.
I think it is important to add a library to our school.		It is important to add a library to North End School.
She quickly got herself together when her mom got there.		She quickly adjusted her behavior when her mom arrived.
Just about everyone thinks that a new band room is the best.		Most of the students surveyed agree that adding a band room would be beneficial.

⟳ YOUR TURN

Identify sentences in your essay that are written with informal language. Then, complete the chart by revising the sentences in a more formal style.

Type of Informal Language	Revision
Contractions	
First Person	
Slang	
Conversational Tone	
Abbreviations	

Skill:
Conclusions

Copyright © BookheadEd Learning, LLC

••• CHECKLIST FOR CONCLUSIONS

Before you write your conclusion, ask yourself the following questions:

- How can I restate the thesis statement in a different way? What impression can I make on my reader?

- How can I write my conclusion so that it supports and follows logically from my argument? Have I left out any important information?

- Should I include a call to action or memorable comment?

Below are two strategies to help you provide a concluding statement or section that follows from and supports the argument presented:

- Peer Discussion

  > After you have written your introduction and body paragraphs, talk with a partner and tell him or her what you want readers to remember, writing notes about your discussion.

  > Review your notes and think about what you wish to express in your conclusion.

- Freewriting

  > Freewrite for ten minutes about what you might include in your conclusion. Don't worry about grammar, punctuation, or having fully formed ideas. The point of freewriting is to discover ideas.

  > Review your notes and think about what you wish to express in your conclusion.

⟳ YOUR TURN

Read the sentences below, taken from the conclusion Cameron's friend wrote. Then, complete the chart by placing each sentence in its correct place in the conclusion outline.

	Sentence Options
A	Adding a photography lab to North End School could change the lives of students. This is a powerful opportunity for our school!
B	Creating a photography lab would help North End build a stronger art program and expose students to a new art medium; research shows that strong art programs correlate to stronger academic scores. A photo lab would also improve our school newspaper and inspire students who are interested in advertising and journalism.
C	Adding a photography lab to North End School would be beneficial.

Conclusion Outline	Sentence
Restate thesis in a different way	
Review and explain your claims	
Call to action or memorable comment	

✎ WRITE

Use the steps in the checklist section to revise the conclusion of your argumentative essay.

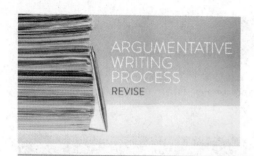

Argumentative Writing Process: Revise

| PLAN | DRAFT | REVISE | EDIT AND PUBLISH |

You have written a draft of your argumentative essay. You have also received input from your peers about how to improve it. Now you are going to revise your draft.

← REVISION GUIDE

Examine your draft to find areas for revision. Keep in mind your purpose and audience as you revise for clarity, development, organization, and style. Use the guide below to help you review:

Review	Revise	Example
Clarity		
Review your thesis statement in your introduction. Identify any places where it can be clearer or more specific.	Use clear and specific language in your thesis statement to preview what your essay will be about. Think about the research you did and consider using academic or formal language.	Overall, we should add a makerspace to North End School because it's a place to create and do experiments, it will help prepare students for ~~jobs in science~~ the STEM jobs of the future, and it is a big opportunity for teachers too.
Development		
Review the development of your claim in the body paragraphs. Identify statements that lack supporting reasons or evidence.	Check off each claim that is supported by reasons and evidence. Add in additional reasons or evidence to statements that need support.	~~The tech and 7th-grade scince teacher think the makerspace and its equippment would help students and their thinking.~~ The technology teacher, Mr. Smith, said that a makerspace would "provide students with the opportunity for a powerful experience to enhance their thinking."

Review	Revise	Example
Organization		
Find places where transitions would improve your essay. Review your body paragraphs to identify and annotate any sentences that don't flow in a clear and logical way.	Rewrite the sentences so they appear in a logical sequence, starting with a clear transition or topic sentence. Delete details that are repetitive or not essential to support the thesis.	~~I think that lots of teachers at North End agree with me. As a school community, we should make sure our students get the very best.~~ In addition to preparing students for the future, North End teachers also think a makerspace would benefit the school and students right now.
Style: Word Choice		
Identify sentences that use informal language. Look for everyday words and phrases that can be replaced with more formal or academic language.	Replace everyday informal language with more formal academic language.	A makerspace at our school can help other students at North End ~~follow~~ pursue interests that can lead to great futures—something we all want.
Style: Sentence Variety		
Read your essay aloud. Annotate places where you have too many long or short sentences in a row.	Rewrite sentences by making them longer or shorter for clarity of emphasis.	Building a makerspace in our school would create a way for students to develop creative skills that would help them in their futures. It would ~~and~~ give them a chance to explore new passions and industries.

✎ WRITE

Use the guide above, as well as your peer reviews, to help you evaluate your argumentative essay to determine areas that should be revised.

Grammar:
Adverb Clauses

Adverb clauses are subordinate clauses that often modify the verb in the main clause of a complex sentence. The can also modify an adjective or adverb.

Adverb clauses tell *when, where, how, why*, or *under what conditions* the action in the main clause occurs.

Adverb clauses begin with subordinating conjunctions.

Common Subordinating Conjunctions				
after although as because	before if since so that	than though unless until	when whenever where whereas	wherever while

Follow these rules when using adverb clauses:

Rule	Text
Use a comma after an introductory adverb clause.	**If you have ever seen a dragon in a pinch,** you will realize that this was only poetical exaggeration applied to any hobbit, even to Old Took's great-granduncle Bullroarer, who was so huge (for a hobbit) that he could ride a horse. The Hobbit
A comma is usually not necessary before an adverb clause that ends a sentence.	"I saw somebody working on it **when we came up this morning.**" The King of Mazy May

↻ YOUR TURN

1. How should this sentence be changed?

   > Everybody ate dessert after they finished eating the main course.

   - ○ A. Insert a comma after the word **dessert**.
   - ○ B. Insert a comma after the word **eating**.
   - ○ C. Insert a comma after the words **dessert** and **eating**.
   - ○ D. No change needs to be made to this sentence.

2. How should this sentence be changed?

   > Since it was just painted, do not lean against the wall.

   - ○ A. Delete the comma after the word **painted**.
   - ○ B. Insert a comma after the word **lean**.
   - ○ C. Delete the comma after the word **painted** and insert a comma after the word **since**.
   - ○ D. No change needs to be made to this sentence.

3. How should this sentence be changed?

   > Whenever I walk to school my cat follows me down the street.

   - ○ A. Insert a comma after the word **walk**.
   - ○ B. Insert a comma after the word **school**.
   - ○ C. Insert a comma after the word **me**.
   - ○ D. No change needs to be made to this sentence.

Grammar: Compound-Complex Sentences

A compound-complex sentence has two or more main clauses and one or more subordinate clauses. It is a combination of a compound sentence and a complex sentence.

A compound sentence has two main clauses. They can be joined by a semicolon or a comma followed by a coordinating conjunction such as *or, and*, or *but*.

A complex sentence has one main clause and one or more subordinate clauses. The main clause and subordinate clause are usually joined with a subordinating conjunction, such as *when, because, before*, or *after*.

Compound-Complex Sentence
The guards had clubs, and they had carbines, too, which they turned around and used as weapons.
The Other Side of the Sky

Main Clause 1	Main Clause 2	Subordinate Clause
The guards had clubs	they had carbines, too	which they turned around and used as weapons.

Subordinating Conjunction	Coordinating Conjunction
which	and

⟳ YOUR TURN

1. How should this sentence be changed so that it becomes a compound-complex sentence?

> You should drain the grease frequently; too much grease is unhealthy.

○ A. Add *when you cook ground beef* after **frequently**.
○ B. Replace the semicolon with a comma and the conjunction *and*.
○ C. Replace the semicolon with a period and remove **too much grease is unhealthy**.
○ D. No change needs to be made to this sentence.

2. How should this sentence be changed so that it becomes a compound-complex sentence?

> We enjoy going to our favorite Mexican restaurant when there is a special deal for groups of six or more, but sometimes we must wait in line for over an hour.

○ A. Delete the comma.
○ B. Replace the comma and conjunction **but** with a semicolon.
○ C. Remove **for over an hour**.
○ D. No change needs to be made to this sentence.

3. How should this sentence be changed so that it becomes a compound-complex sentence?

> Whether it is summer or winter, the weather often goes below freezing here.

○ A. Replace **whether** with *when*.
○ B. Add a semicolon after **here** and add *you will need to buy a warmer coat*.
○ C. Remove **whether it is summer or winter**.
○ D. No change needs to be made to this sentence.

4. How should this sentence be changed so that it becomes a compound-complex sentence?

> Roses and tulips grow and bloom in the garden.

○ A. Add *when it's spring* after **garden**.
○ B. Add *when it's spring* before **roses** and add a semicolon after **garden** followed by *I plant them in the fall*.
○ C. Add a semicolon after **garden** and then add *I plant them in the fall*.
○ D. No change needs to be made to this sentence.

Grammar:
Basic Spelling Rules II

Doubled Consonants

Spelling Conventions	Correct Spelling	Incorrect Spelling
Before adding -*ed* or a suffix: When a one-syllable word ends in one consonant following one vowel, double the final consonant.	slap + -*ed* = slapped jog + -*er* = jogger	slaped joger
Double the final consonant if the last syllable of the word is accented and the accent stays there after the suffix is added.	omit + -*ed* = omitted occur + -*ence* = occurrence infer + -*ing* = inferring	omited occurence infering
Before adding -*ly* to a double *l*: When adding -*ly* to a word that ends in *ll*, drop one *l*.	full + -*ly* = fully chill + -*ly* = chilly	fullly chilly

Compound Words

Spelling Conventions	Original Words	Compound Words
When forming compound words, maintain all original spellings.	snow + storm broad + cast	snowstorm broadcast

Spelling -*cede*, -*ceed*, and -*sede*

Spelling Conventions	Correct Spelling	Incorrect Spelling
The only English word ending in -*sede* is *supersede*.	supersede	superceed
Three words end in -*ceed: proceed, exceed,* and *succeed*.	proceed exceed succeed	procede exsede succede
All other words ending with the "seed" sound are spelled with -*cede*.	precede recede secede	preceed receed sesede

↻ YOUR TURN

1. How should the spelling error in this sentence be corrected?

> The ground was littered on the 5th of July because no one had disposed of their wrapers after the fireworks.

- ○ A. Change **wrapers** to **wrappers and firworks to fireworks**.
- ○ B. Change **wrapers** to **wrappers**.
- ○ C. Change **firworks** to **fireworks**.
- ○ D. No change needs to be made to this sentence.

2. How should the spelling error in this sentence be corrected?

> This year's ticket sales far excede those for previous years because the community is fully committed to saving the theater program.

- ○ A. Change **excede** to **exceed**.
- ○ B. Change **fully** to **fullly**.
- ○ C. Change **committed** to **commited**.
- ○ D. No change needs to be made to this sentence.

3. How should the spelling error in this sentence be corrected?

> He finally admitted that the evidence was not compeling enough to make an airtight case.

- ○ A. Change **admitted** to **admited**.
- ○ B. Change **compeling** to **compelling**.
- ○ C. Change **airtight** to **air-tight**.
- ○ D. No change needs to be made to this sentence.

4. How should the spelling error in this sentence be corrected?

> She often remembered her grandfather's story fondly, and proceeded to share it with her own granddaughters when they were old enough.

- ○ A. Change **grandfather's** to **grand father's**.
- ○ B. Change **proceeded** to **proceded**.
- ○ C. Change **granddaughters** to **grandaughters**.
- ○ D. No change needs to be made to this sentence.

Argumentative Writing Process: Edit and Publish

PLAN	DRAFT	REVISE	EDIT AND PUBLISH

You have revised your argumentative essay based on your peer feedback and your own examination.

Now, it is time to edit your essay. When you revised, you focused on the content of your essay. You probably looked at the thesis statement, reasons and relevant evidence, introduction, and conclusion. When you edit, you should focus on grammar and punctuation.

Use the checklist below to guide you as you edit:

- [ ] Have I used adverb clauses correctly?

- [ ] Have I used compound-complex sentences correctly?

- [ ] Do I have any sentence fragments or run-on sentences?

- [ ] Have I spelled everything correctly?

Notice some edits Cameron has made:

- Created a compound-complex sentence by adding a subordinate clause and a coordinating conjunction.

- Used an adverb clause to tell when.

- Fixed spelling errors.

In addition to preparing students for the future, North End teachers also think a makerspace would benefit the school and students right now. Because a makerspace can be used in many ways, teachers ~~Teachers~~ in multiple subjects could use a makerspace for special projects in science, art, and math. ~~They~~, and they could also use it for an ~~after school~~ after-school club. Before last semester ended, interviews ~~Interviews~~ were conducted with several teachers at North End. The technology teacher, Mr. Smith, said that a makerspace would "provide students with the opportunity for a powerful experience to enhance their thinking." Ms. Bo, the 7th-grade ~~scince~~ science teacher, said that "the addition of a makerspace and its ~~equippment~~ equipment would foster creativity, tinkering, and curiosity, which leads to better thinking and better questioning." This clearly shows that teachers think a makerspace would improve the quality of their classes and student thinking.

✏ WRITE

Use the questions on the previous page, as well as your peer reviews, to help you evaluate your argumentative essay to determine areas that need editing. Then edit your essay to correct those errors.

Once you have made all your corrections, you are ready to publish your work. You can distribute your writing to family and friends, hang it on a bulletin board, or post it on your blog. If you publish online, share the link with your family, friends, and classmates.

Please note that excerpts and passages in the StudySync® library and this workbook are intended as touchstones to generate interest in an author's work. The excerpts and passages do not substitute for the reading of entire texts, and StudySync® strongly recommends that students seek out and purchase the whole literary or informational work in order to experience it as the author intended. Links to online resellers are available in our digital library. In addition, complete works may be ordered through an authorized reseller by filling out and returning to StudySync® the order form enclosed in this workbook.

Reading & Writing
Companion

125

Taking A Stand

INFORMATIONAL TEXT

Introduction

Bullying is a widespread problem, and it can happen anywhere—in school, during activities, or online. This article, "Taking a Stand," details seventh-grader Isabella Petrini's decision to speak out against bullying. Once a bully herself, Petrini started an anti-bullying program at her school. Through it she convinced many others to stop being mean and start trying to understand

V VOCABULARY

bullying
using strength or power to get what you want or to make someone feel bad

platform
type of computer hardware or software; operating system

aggressive
prepared and eager to fight or disagree

pledge
written promise

digital
using electronic or computer technology

≡ READ

NOTES

1 Imagine a bad day at school. Maybe you got to class and heard muffled giggling. Maybe you heard buzzing whispers in the hall. Maybe later at home you wept blinding tears.

2 Students often worry about studying and sports at school. But for many students, something is more worrisome: **bullying**. Bullying is "unwanted or **aggressive** behavior." It can happen face to face. Or it can happen through **digital platforms** such as texting and social media.

3 In 2014, almost 30 percent of students said they'd been bullied. Many don't report the bullying. More than 60 percent stay silent. They endure the sickening fear of being bullied. They feel as though no one can help.

4 Bullying has costs. Bullied students are more likely to have health problems like depression and anxiety. They are more likely to struggle in school. Some become bullies themselves.

Please note that excerpts and passages in the StudySync® library and this workbook are intended as touchstones to generate interest in an author's work. The excerpts and passages do not substitute for the reading of entire texts, and StudySync® strongly recommends that students seek out and purchase the whole literary or informational work in order to experience it as the author intended. Links to online resellers are available in our digital library. In addition, complete works may be ordered through an authorized reseller by filling out and returning to StudySync® the order form enclosed in this workbook.

Reading & Writing Companion 127

5   Isabella Petrini knows about bullying. In fifth grade, she was a bully. She and her friends said mean things about others. But in seventh grade, Petrini saw bullying differently. She realized that these comments weren't jokes. They were biting and hurtful. They had the potential to harm others.

6   When Petrini saw the television program *If You Really Knew Me*, she had an idea. On the program, real-life high school students come together and talk about bullying. The goal is to help stop bullying by helping people understand one another.

7   The program turned Petrini into an activist. She wanted to begin an anti-bullying initiative at her school. She and her friends agreed that school could be a better place. People needed to accept one another instead of making stinging insults or passing silent judgment.

8   The girls made a plan. They shared it with the principal. He supported their idea. They organized a school assembly. Petrini showed part of *If You Really Knew Me*. People watched with wide-eyed attention. Students were asked to sign a **pledge** to help stop bullying. The program was popular. Students liked that it was started by students.

9   Petrini and her friends continued their fight. They joined with others in school. Together, they came up with ideas like no-bullying zones. They focused on understanding others and standing up to bullying.

First Read

Read the text. After you read, answer the Think Questions below.

☁ THINK QUESTIONS

1. What is bullying?

   Bullying is _____.

2. What are two ways bullying can hurt a student?

   Two ways bullying can hurt a student are _____

   _____.

3. What did Petrini and her friends do to take a stand against bullying at their school? Cite evidence from the text to support your answer.

   Petrini and her friends _____

   _____.

4. Use context to confirm the meaning of the word *pledge* as it is used in "Taking a Stand." Write your definition of *pledge* here.

   Pledge means _____.

   A context clue is _____.

5. What is another way to say that some of the students are *aggressive*?

   Some of the students _____.

Skill: Analyzing Expressions

★ DEFINE

When you read, you may find English expressions that you do not know. An **expression** is a group of words that communicates an idea. Three types of expressions are idioms, sayings, and figurative language. They can be difficult to understand because the meanings of the words are different from their **literal**, or usual, meanings.

An **idiom** is an expression that is commonly known among a group of people. For example: "It's raining cats and dogs" means it is raining heavily. **Sayings** are short expressions that contain advice or wisdom. For instance: "Don't count your chickens before they hatch" means do not plan on something good happening before it happens. **Figurative** language is when you describe something by comparing it with something else, either directly (using the words *like* or *as*) or indirectly. For example, "I'm as hungry as a horse" means I'm very hungry. None of the expressions are about actual animals.

••• CHECKLIST FOR ANALYZING EXPRESSIONS

To determine the meaning of an expression, remember the following:

✓ If you find a confusing group of words, it may be an expression. The meaning of words in expressions may not be their literal meaning.

- Ask yourself: Is this confusing because the words are new? Or because the words do not make sense together?

✓ Determining the overall meaning may require that you use one or more of the following:

- context clues
- a dictionary or other resource
- teacher or peer support

✓ Highlight important information before and after the expression to look for clues.

YOUR TURN

Read the following excerpt from the text. Then, complete the multiple-choice questions below.

---

from "Taking a Stand"

The girls made a plan. They shared it with the principal. He supported their idea. They organized a school assembly. Petrini showed part of *If You Really Knew Me*. People watched with wide-eyed attention. Students were asked to sign a pledge to help stop bullying. The program was popular. Students liked that it was started by students.

Petrini and her friends continued their fight. They joined with others in school. Together, they came up with ideas like no-bullying zones. They focused on understanding others and standing up to bullying.

---

1. What does "standing up to" bullying mean in this text?

    ○ A. Petrini and her friends are not sitting in their seats.

    ○ B. Petrini and her friends are trying to stop bullying.

    ○ C. Petrini and her friends are supporting bullying.

    ○ D. Petrini and her friends are walking away from bullying.

2. Which context clue helped you determine the meaning of the expression?

    ○ A. "He supported their idea."

    ○ B. "People watched with wide-eyed attention."

    ○ C. "Students liked that it was started by students."

    ○ D. "Together, they came up with ideas like no-bullying zones."

Please note that excerpts and passages in the StudySync® library and this workbook are intended as touchstones to generate interest in an author's work. The excerpts and passages do not substitute for the reading of entire texts, and StudySync® strongly recommends that students seek out and purchase the whole literary or informational work in order to experience it as the author intended. Links to online resellers are available in our digital library. In addition, complete works may be ordered through an authorized reseller by filling out and returning to StudySync® the order form enclosed in this workbook.

Reading & Writing Companion   **131**

Skill:
Main Ideas and Details

★ DEFINE

The **main ideas** are the most important ideas of a paragraph, a section, or an entire text. The **supporting details** are details that describe or explain the main idea.

To **identify** the main idea of a paragraph or a text, you need to decide what the text is mostly about. To **identify** supporting details, you need to decide what information describes or explains the main idea.

••• CHECKLIST FOR MAIN IDEAS AND DETAILS

In order to distinguish between main ideas and supporting details, do the following:

✓ Preview the text. Look at headings, topic sentences, and boldface vocabulary.

- Ask yourself: What is this text about?

✓ Read the text.

- Ask yourself: What are the most important ideas? What details support or explain the most important ideas?

✓ Take notes or use a graphic organizer to distinguish between main ideas and supporting details.

↻ YOUR TURN

Read paragraphs 5–6 from the text. Then, complete the multiple-choice questions below.

---

from **"Taking a Stand"**

Isabella Petrini knows about bullying. In fifth grade, she was a bully. She and her friends said mean things about others. But in seventh grade, Petrini saw bullying differently. She realized that these comments weren't jokes. They were biting and hurtful. They had the potential to harm others.

When Petrini saw the television program *If You Really Knew Me*, she had an idea. On the program, real-life high school students come together and talk about bullying. The goal is to help stop bullying by helping people understand one another.

---

1. What is the main idea of paragraph 5?

    ○ A. Isabella Petrini is a bully.
    ○ B. Isabella Petrini knows that bullying is harmful.
    ○ C. Bullies' comments are jokes.
    ○ D. Bullies are not harmful to other students until the students are in seventh grade.

2. What is a detail that supports the main idea of paragraph 5?

    ○ A. Petrini's friends in fifth grade were bullies.
    ○ B. Petrini was a bully in fifth grade.
    ○ C. Petrini said mean things in fifth grade.
    ○ D. Petrini realized that her comments could hurt people.

3. What is the main idea of paragraph 6?

    ○ A. The anti-bullying program *If You Really Knew Me* inspired Isabella Petrini.
    ○ B. Isabella Petrini made a TV program to teach students how to stop bullying.
    ○ C. *If You Really Knew Me* is about educating bullies like Isabella Petrini.
    ○ D. Isabella Petrini watched a TV program called *If You Really Knew Me*.

4. What is a detail that supports the main idea of paragraph 6?

    ○ A. She had an idea.
    ○ B. real-life high school students
    ○ C. come together
    ○ D. talk about bullying

Close Read

✏ WRITE

INFORMATIONAL: Write text for a flyer to inform students about bullying in school and why it is a problem. Use information from the selection to support your ideas. Pay attention to the spelling rules for doubling the final consonants and adding prefixes as you write.

Use the checklist below to guide you as you write.

☐ Why is bullying a problem?

☐ What can people do to solve this problem?

☐ What information from the text supports your ideas?

Use the sentence frames to organize and write your informational flyer.

• Bullying is _____

_____.

• As many as 30% of students _____

_____.

• Bullying causes _____

_____.

• We need to stop bullying because _____

_____.

• People can put an end to bullying by _____

_____.

School Lunches:

Who Decides What Students Should Eat?

ARGUMENTATIVE TEXT

Introduction

In these two articles, writers make arguments for and against healthful school lunch programs. One writer argues that healthful school lunch programs benefit students. The other argues that taking away unhealthful options also takes away students' power of choice. After reading their arguments, what will you decide? Should schools determine what students eat for lunch, or should students have the final say?

 VOCABULARY

healthful

having qualities that help make someone healthy; good for you

bitter

having a harsh, unpleasant taste

tart

having a sharp or sour taste

soggy

soaked

hearty

filling; satisfying

NOTES

≡ READ

School Lunches: Who Decides What Students Should Eat?

Point: New Programs Give Healthful Options

1 School lunches have changed in the United States. Many groups advocate for more **healthful** lunches. They work hard to change the kinds of food students eat at school. They want students to eat more healthful foods. They suggest whole grains, fruits, and vegetables.

2 When the new school lunch programs started, many students were reluctant to try the new foods. They did not want to eat crunchy carrots and juicy oranges. They wanted to eat salty chips and sweet cookies. But the protests got quieter. Now, students happily eat the healthful foods. Many schools even have salad bars. Students can make their own salads. They have a lot of options. Students can top crispy lettuce with **tart** tomatoes, **hearty** black beans, or sweet peaches. Now, students embrace healthful foods.

NOTES

3   Healthful school lunches benefit students at lunch. They also benefit students the rest of the day. Research shows that students who eat more healthful lunches eat less sugar and are more physically active. For the good of our students—our most valuable resource—our schools should have healthful lunches.

Counterpoint: New Rules Limit Student Choice

4   Many groups want to change what students eat during school lunch. They want to take away pizza, chips, and soda. Instead, they want students to eat salads, whole wheat pasta, and other healthful foods. They say that these changes will make students healthier and stronger.

5   But these changes cause problems. Many students don't like the more healthful foods. They say these foods don't taste good. After all, nobody wants to eat **bitter**, **soggy** broccoli instead of chicken nuggets! Students throw away a lot of the healthful foods. Then they are hungry by the end of the day. When students are hungry, they are more tired and more distracted in class.

6   Because of the rules, students don't have many choices. They don't have the right to choose what they eat. Some schools have banned the sale of chips, candy, and soda. Students can't even get these foods from school vending machines. Many say that this lack of choice takes away students' rights. Who should have the power to choose which foods are on lunch trays: schools or the students who have to eat those foods?

Please note that excerpts and passages in the StudySync® library and this workbook are intended as touchstones to generate interest in an author's work. The excerpts and passages do not substitute for the reading of entire texts, and StudySync® strongly recommends that students seek out and purchase the whole literary or informational work in order to experience it as the author intended. Links to online resellers are available in our digital library. In addition, complete works may be ordered through an authorized reseller by filling out and returning to StudySync® the order form enclosed in this workbook.

Reading & Writing
Companion

137

First Read

Read the text. After you read, answer the Think Questions below.

☁ THINK QUESTIONS

1. What is the goal of more healthful school lunch programs?

   The goal of the more healthful school lunch programs is _____

   _____ .

2. According to the text, what are some benefits of more healthful school lunch programs? Cite evidence from the text in your response.

   Some benefits of the programs are _____ .

3. Why do some people argue against healthful school lunch programs? Cite evidence from the text in your response.

   Some people argue against the programs _____ .

4. Use context to confirm the meaning of the word *soggy* as it is used in "School Lunches: Who Decides What Students Should Eat?" Write your definition of *soggy* here.

   Soggy means _____ .

   A context clue is _____ .

5. What is another way to say that a meal is *hearty*?

   A meal is _____ .

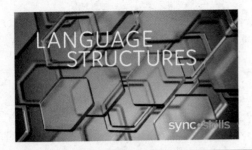

Skill:
Language Structures

★ DEFINE

In every language, there are rules that tell how to **structure** sentences. These rules define the correct order of words. In the English language, for example, a **basic** structure for sentences is subject, verb, and object. Some sentences have more **complicated** structures.

You will encounter both basic and complicated **language structures** in the classroom materials you read. Being familiar with language structures will help you better understand the text.

••• CHECKLIST FOR LANGUAGE STRUCTURES

To improve your comprehension of language structures, do the following:

✓ Monitor your understanding.

- Ask yourself: Why do I not understand this sentence? Is it because I do not understand some of the words? Or is it because I do not understand the way the words are ordered in the sentence?

✓ Pay attention to coordinating conjunctions.

- **Coordinating conjunctions** are used to join words or groups of words that have equal grammatical importance.

  > The coordinating conjunction *and* shows that two or more things are true of a person, object, or event.
  Example: Josefina is a good athlete **and** student.

  > The coordinating conjunction *or* shows a choice between different possibilities.
  Example: Josefina can either do her homework **or** go for a run.

Please note that excerpts and passages in the StudySync® library and this workbook are intended as touchstones to generate interest in an author's work. The excerpts and passages do not substitute for the reading of entire texts, and StudySync® strongly recommends that students seek out and purchase the whole literary or informational work in order to experience it as the author intended. Links to online resellers are available in our digital library. In addition, complete works may be ordered through an authorized reseller by filling out and returning to StudySync® the order form enclosed in this workbook.

Reading & Writing Companion   **139**

> The coordinating conjunction *but* shows a contrast between people, objects, or events.
> Example: Josefina wants to run **but** should finish her homework first.

✓ Break down the sentence into its parts.

- Ask yourself: What ideas are expressed in this sentence? Are there conjunctions that join ideas or show contrast?

✓ Confirm your understanding with a peer or teacher.

⟳ YOUR TURN

Read each sentence in the first column. Place the letter that identifies the correct coordinating conjunction in the middle column. Place the letter that describes what each conjunction shows in the last column.

Coordinating Conjunction	Shows . . .
A. and	D. a contrast between what will happen
B. but	E. a choice between the options
C. or	F. two things are true about students

Sentence	Coordinating Conjunction	Shows . . .
Students can top crispy lettuce with tart tomatoes, hearty black beans, or sweet peaches.		
These changes will make students healthier, but these changes cause problems.		
Students are more tired and more distracted in class.		

Skill:
Comparing and Contrasting

★ DEFINE

To **compare** is to show how two or more pieces of information or literary elements in a text are similar. To **contrast** is to show how two or more pieces of information or literary elements in a text are different. By comparing and contrasting, you can better understand the **meaning** and the **purpose** of the text you are reading.

••• CHECKLIST FOR COMPARING AND CONTRASTING

In order to compare and contrast, do the following:

✓ Look for information or elements that you can compare and contrast.

- Ask yourself: How are these two things similar? How are they different?

✓ Look for signal words that indicate a compare-and-contrast relationship.

- Ask yourself: Are there any words that indicate the writer is trying to compare and contrast two or more things?

✓ Use a graphic organizer, such as a Venn diagram or chart, to compare and contrast information.

YOUR TURN

Read the following excerpts from the text. Then, complete the Compare-and-Contrast chart by writing the letter of the correct example in chart below.

Excerpt 1:

Healthful school lunches benefit students at lunch. They also benefit students the rest of the day. Research shows that students who eat more healthful lunches eat less sugar and are more physically active. For the good of our students—our most valuable resource—our schools should have healthful lunches.

Excerpt 2:

But these changes cause problems. Many students don't like the more healthful foods. They say these foods don't taste good. After all, nobody wants to eat bitter, soggy broccoli instead of chicken nuggets! Students throw away a lot of the healthful foods. Then they are hungry by the end of the day. When students are hungry, they are more tired and more distracted in class.

	Examples
A	If students are hungry, they are tired and distracted.
B	Eating healthy can help students be more physically active.
C	Food can affect how students behave in school.

Healthful Options Are Good	Both	Healthful Options Are Bad

Close Read

✏ WRITE

ARGUMENTATIVE: One author argues that more healthful school lunches benefit students. Another author argues that such programs limit students' choices. Which argument do you agree with? Explain why you agree with the argument. Pay attention to verb tenses as you write.

Use the checklist below to guide you as you write.

☐ Which author do you agree with?

☐ How did that author convince you?

☐ What personal experience supports your view?

Use the sentence frames to organize and write your argument.

The first author believes that healthful lunches are _____.

The second author thinks that these programs are _____.

I agree with the (first / second) _____ author. I think that _____

_____.

The author's statement that "_____"

was very convincing. Personally, I _____.

PHOTO/IMAGE CREDITS:

studysync®

Text Fulfillment Through StudySync

If you are interested in specific titles, please fill out the form below and we will check availability through our partners.

ORDER DETAILS

Date:

TITLE	AUTHOR	Paperback/ Hardcover	Specific Edition *If Applicable*	Quantity

SHIPPING INFORMATION

Contact:

Title:

School/District:

Address Line 1:

Address Line 2:

Zip or Postal Code:

Phone:

Mobile:

Email:

BILLING INFORMATION   ☐ *SAME AS SHIPPING*

Contact:

Title:

School/District:

Address Line 1:

Address Line 2:

Zip or Postal Code:

Phone:

Mobile:

Email:

PAYMENT INFORMATION

☐ CREDIT CARD

Name on Card:

Card Number: Expiration Date: Security Code:

☐ PO

Purchase Order Number:

StudySync Text Fulfillment, BookheadEd Learning, LLC
610 Daniel Young Drive | Sonoma, CA 95476